SCIENTISTS OF

Wales and the Bomb

SCIENTISTS OF WALES

Wales and the Bomb

THE ROLE OF WELSH SCIENTISTS AND ENGINEERS IN THE BRITISH NUCLEAR PROGRAMME

JOHN BAYLIS

UNIVERSITY OF WALES PRESS
2019

www.uwp.co.uk

British Library Cataloguing-in-Publication Data
A catalogue record for this book is available from the British Library.

ISBN   978-1-78683-359-4
eISBN   978-1-78683-360-0

The right of John Baylis to be identified as author of this work has been asserted in accordance with sections 77, 78 and 79 of the Copyright, Designs and Patents Act 1988.

The publisher acknowledges the financial support of the Welsh Books Council.

THE LEARNED SOCIETY OF WALES
CYMDEITHAS DDYSGEDIG CYMRU

MIX
Paper from
responsible sources
FSC FSC® C013604

Typeset by Marie Doherty
Printed by CPI Antony Rowe, Melksham.

*This book is dedicated to Marion for her love
and support over more than fifty years*

CONTENTS

SERIES EDITOR'S FOREWORD

Wales has a long and important history of contributions to scientific and technological discovery and innovation stretching from the Middle Ages to the present day. From medieval scholars to contemporary scientists and engineers, Welsh individuals have been at the forefront of efforts to understand and control the world around us. For much of Welsh history, science has played a key role in Welsh culture: bards drew on scientific ideas in their poetry; renaissance gentlemen devoted themselves to natural history; the leaders of early Welsh Methodism filled their hymns with scientific references. During the nineteenth century, scientific societies flourished and Wales was transformed by engineering and technology. In the twentieth century the work of Welsh scientists continued to influence developments in their fields.

Much of this exciting and vibrant Welsh scientific history has now disappeared from historical memory. The aim of the Scientists of Wales series is to resurrect the role of science and technology in Welsh history. Its volumes trace the careers and achievements of Welsh investigators, setting their work within their cultural contexts. They demonstrate how scientists and engineers have contributed to the making of modern Wales as well as showing the ways in which Wales has played a crucial role in the emergence of modern science and engineering.

RHAGAIR GOLYGYDD
Y GYFRES

O'r Oesoedd Canol hyd heddiw, mae gan Gymru hanes hir a phwysig o gyfrannu at ddarganfyddiadau a menter gwyddonol a thechnolegol. O'r ysgolheigion cynharaf i wyddonwyr a pheirianwyr cyfoes, mae Cymry wedi bod yn flaenllaw yn yr ymdrech i ddeall a rheoli'r byd o'n cwmpas. Mae gwyddoniaeth wedi chwarae rôl allweddol o fewn diwylliant Cymreig am ran helaeth o hanes Cymru: arferai'r beirdd llys dynnu ar syniadau gwyddonol yn eu barddoniaeth; roedd gan wŷr y Dadeni ddiddordeb brwd yn y gwyddorau naturiol; ac roedd emynau arweinwyr cynnar Methodistiaeth Gymreig yn llawn cyfeiriadau gwyddonol. Blodeuodd cymdeithasau gwyddonol yn ystod y bedwaredd ganrif ar bymtheg, a thrawsffurfiwyd Cymru gan beirianneg a thechnoleg. Ac, yn ogystal, bu gwyddonwyr Cymreig yn ddylanwadol mewn sawl maes gwyddonol a thechnolegol yn yr ugeinfed ganrif.

Mae llawer o'r hanes gwyddonol Cymreig cyffrous yma wedi hen ddiflannu. Amcan cyfres Gwyddonwyr Cymru yw i danlinellu cyfraniad gwyddoniaeth a thechnoleg yn hanes Cymru, â'i chyfrolau'n olrhain gyrfaoedd a champau gwyddonwyr Cymreig gan osod eu gwaith yn ei gyd-destun diwylliannol. Trwy ddangos sut y cyfrannodd gwyddonwyr a pheirianwyr at greu'r Gymru fodern, dadlennir hefyd sut y mae Cymru wedi chwarae rhan hanfodol yn natblygiad gwyddoniaeth a pheirianneg fodern.

LIST OF ILLUSTRATIONS

ACKNOWLEDGEMENTS

I am very grateful to a number of people and institutions who have helped at various stages to bring this book to fruition. I owe a great debt to Professor John Tucker of Swansea University. Having written a paper for the Learned Society of Wales (LSW) on the topic covered by the book, Professor Tucker, in his capacity as the history of science and technology coordinator of the LSW, provided great encouragement to turn the paper into a book for the Scientists of Wales series. Professor Tucker also helped to secure some funding towards the publication of the book. In particular, I would like to thank the Learned Society of Wales, the South Wales Institute of Engineers Educational Trust, Swansea University, and the Welsh Books Council for very generously providing the financial support without which it would not have been possible for the book to have been published.

I am also grateful to Dr Richard Moore who helped set up interviews with some Welsh scientists at Aldermaston and to Dr Kristan Stoddart for allowing me to use some of the material from joint research that was included in two articles published in the journal *Diplomacy and Statecraft*. There are a number of images included in the book and I would like to thank the following for permissions to reproduce the photographs, tables and diagrams: The Royal Society; English Public Health; and Washington University in St Louis, USA. I am particularly grateful to Brian Burnell for making a number of drawings specifically for me that are included in the book. I would also like to thank Alwyn Davies, Alex Wellerstein, Jane Hughes, Barbara Jones, Professor Mike Charlton, Dr Colin Barber and Professor Len Scott for invaluable information and advice at various times during the writing of this book. Finally, my thanks go to Llion Wigley and Dafydd Jones of the University of Wales Press for all their help and assistance at various stages in the publication of the book.

PREFACE

Nuclear weapons pose very difficult ethical, scientific, engineering and industrial problems. Given the continuing contemporary debate about the utility or otherwise of nuclear weapons, it is interesting to look back at the evolution of the British nuclear programme. It is a fascinating story in which Wales, and some of its leading scientists and engineers, played a significant role in developing atomic and later thermonuclear weapons. For some this may be a surprise given that anti-establishment feelings and pacifism have traditionally been strong forces in Welsh nonconformity and radicalism, especially amongst members of the Welsh nationalist movement.[1] For others this is less of a surprise given the support for nuclear weapons in sectors of the Labour Party and an undercurrent of conservative values in Welsh society more generally.[2]

My interest in this subject began in the late 1980s when I attended the inaugural meeting of the British Nuclear History Programme. At that meeting I met for the first time the two official historians of the British nuclear weapons programme, Professor Margaret Gowing and Lorna Arnold. In conversation Professor Gowing noticed my accent and asked if I was Welsh. I said I was and she said that from her research she had been surprised by how many Welsh scientists and engineers had been involved in the early atomic energy programme. She suggested that this was something that deserved further research. Over the years I got to know Lorna Arnold well and in conference meetings and fairly regular telephone conversations we discussed aspects of the British nuclear programme and she often raised the issue of the role of Welsh scientists and engineers.

As part of the nuclear history programme I wrote a book for Oxford University Press entitled *Ambiguity and Deterrence: British Nuclear Strategy 1945–1964* in which I tried to follow the example of Margaret Gowing and Lorna Arnold in their publications in dealing with some of the key personalities in the British nuclear programme.[3] After the publication of this book Lorna Arnold encouraged me once again to do some further work on the role of Welsh scientists and engineers in the programme. At the time, however, I was more interested in the wider British nuclear programme and the politics, strategy and ethics of nuclear weapons more generally. As time went on I also became more involved with university administration which gave me less and less time for research. When I retired, however, I renewed my interest in the subject and started to discover that there were both scientists and facilities in Wales that played a much more important role in the development of atomic energy, for civilian use, but especially for military purposes, than I had ever realised. The more research I did, the more I realised that Welsh scientists and engineers played not only an important role in the early nuclear programme but also in further developments from the 1960s through to the present day.

As with my previous studies on nuclear history I have found the journey that has led to this book both fascinating but also at times inevitably rather frustrating. The documents offer some, but rarely all, of the historical record. Many of the scientists and engineers are no longer around to tell their stories. Those that are still alive are often eager to explain the role they played in some of the major scientific discoveries and events of the twentieth century. However, the Official Secrets Act prevents them from telling their stories in full. Nevertheless, from a variety of sources, including some interviews and correspondence with some of the Welsh scientists and engineers involved, it has been possible to produce, at least, a partial picture of the roll of 'taffy's men' in the British nuclear programme. I do not claim that this is a complete picture of the contribution of all of the Welsh scientists and engineers involved in the atomic energy programme. Nor do I claim to have a complete understanding of everything that the scientists and engineers mentioned in the following pages contributed to the British nuclear programme.

This is partly because of the Official Secrets Act and partly because of my own inadequacies. I am a historian and social scientist by training, with only an amateur's understanding of the natural sciences. I have been helped by a number of friends who are scientists, but the mistakes that occur in the pages that follow are my own.

John Baylis
Mumbles, 2018

1

INTRODUCTION

A brief history of atomic energy research

We now know a great deal about the science and technology of atomic energy. We know that atoms are constructed like miniature solar systems. At the centre of the atom is the nucleus, with electrons orbiting around it. We know that the nucleus is made up of protons and neutrons, packed together very tightly. Hydrogen, the lightest element has one proton while uranium, the heaviest natural element, has ninety-two protons. We also know that the nucleus is held together with great force, indeed it is 'the strongest force in nature'. We now know also that when it is bombarded with a neutron, it can split apart in a process called fission. We know that because uranium nuclei are so large, the nuclear force that binds them together is relatively weak, making uranium good for fission. In the fission process excess neutrons are released which can trigger a chain reaction causing a massive release of energy.[1]

All of this knowledge however was the result of the work of many philosophers and scientists going as far back as the Greek philosopher, Leucippus and his pupil, Democritus, in the fifth century BC. It was Democritus who first used the word 'atom', meaning 'not divisible', to define the smallest constituent of matter. It was not, however, until the seventeenth and eighteenth centuries that more scientific ideas about the atom emerged. Isaac Newton, the greatest scientist of his day, argued in his *Optics* that matter was formed in solid, hard, impenetrable Particles. In the nineteenth century John Dalton, a British chemist, wrote a book entitled *A New System of Chemical Philosophy* in which he argued that elements are formed from certain combinations of atoms and that all atoms of the same element are identical.[2] Dalton also believed that atoms were hard indestructible spheres, like billiard balls. He saw chemical compounds as simple geometrical arrangements of these spheres.[3]

The next major development in atomic theory came with Faraday's work in 1833–4 on the effects resulting from the passage of electricity through a solution of a chemical compound. This led him to the conclusion that associated with each atom in solution is a definite quantity of electricity which is the same for the atoms of all elements. Some years later Johnstone Stoney argued that Faraday's work had shown that electricity exists in separate portions, atoms of electricity, to which he gave the name electron. This opened up ideas in the scientific community in the 1880s that there was a common unit of electric charge and that atoms had some kind of structure which might mean that, contrary to previous thinking, they might not be impenetrable.

The 1890s were a particularly productive era for atomic theory. In 1897 J. J. Thomson of the Cavendish laboratory in Cambridge published evidence that proved the existence of a negatively charged particle with a mass about one two-thousandth of that of a hydrogen atom. These particles, now known as electrons, demonstrated the existence of an entity common to all matter, a building block for atoms. Two years earlier Wilhelm Roentgen in Germany was experimenting with cathode rays in a glass tube in which a discharge was taking place when he noticed that radiation was emitted that was capable of penetrating opaque objects. He called this radiation x-rays. The fluorescent effect associated with x-rays led a French scientist, Henri Becquerel, in 1896 to study the fluorescent salts of the element uranium. He found that the salts emitted radiation and that the radiation belonged to the element uranium itself. Marie Curie gave the name radioactivity to this property of spontaneously emitting ionising radiation. Marie Curie and her husband Pierre went on to do further research on uranium and in 1898 they isolated two new elements that exhibited spontaneous energy production: polonium and radium.

At much the same time Ernest Rutherford, working initially in Cambridge and then at McGill University in Montreal, was working on the radiations emitted by uranium. He discovered that there were two types of rays which he called alpha and beta rays. The alpha rays are streams of heavy, positively charged particles which emerge from the radioactive atoms with great energy, but are not very penetrating. Beta rays are also streams of particles, (electrons) light in weight, negatively charged and moderately penetrating, which could be stopped by a thin sheet of metal.[4] At the same time a French scientist, Paul Ulrich Villard, discovered gamma rays. These are electromagnetic waves, similar to x-rays, which are very penetrating and can only be stopped by lead or a similar heavy material.

In 1900 Rutherford began work with Frederick Soddy from Oxford. By studying the nature of radioactivity they reached the revolutionary conclusion that atoms were not indestructible. After returning to Manchester University in 1907 Rutherford continued his experiments with alpha particles and in 1909 undertook one of the crucial experiments in physics, investigating the extent to which a beam of alpha particles is spread out after passing through thin metal foil.[5] The results led Rutherford to propose a nuclear model of the atom. His idea 'was that the atom consisted of a central positively-charged nucleus in which most of the mass of the atom is concentrated, surrounded by a distribution of electrons'.[6] In 1917 he succeeded his old Professor J. J. Thomson in the Cavendish chair in Cambridge where he continued his work exploring the structure of the nucleus. Working with James Chadwick in 1920 he highlighted the importance of the hydrogen nucleus in the structure of atoms which he called the proton.

Rutherford also speculated about the possible existence of an uncharged entity which could explain gamma radiation. It was James Chadwick, however, in 1932 who discovered the neutron. Research by Bothe and Becker in 1930 involving the alpha particle bombardment of certain light elements resulted in the emission of a penetrating radiation which they took to be gamma radiation. Chadwick realised that the radiation was more penetrating than any known hitherto and was able to establish that it was made up of particles of mass nearly equal to that of the proton and with no net charge. As Margaret Gowing has pointed out, 'with the discovery of the neutron the picture of the structure of the atom took the form that it still has, in essence, today. The miniature solar system … (in which) the nucleus is made up of protons and neutrons', with electrons circulating around it.[7]

Chadwick's discovery of the neutron led to experiments by Enrico Fermi in Rome in which he demonstrated that artificial radioactivity could be produced by bombarding even the heaviest elements with neutrons. In 1934 he found that one of the elements that could be activated by neutron bombardment was uranium, the heaviest naturally occurring element. Fermi's experiments were followed up by a number of other scientists, including Lise Meitner, Otto Hahn, Frederic and Irene Joliot-Curie, Fritz Strassmann, Otto Frisch and Niels Bohr. Meitner was forced to leave Germany in July 1938 because of Hitler's persecution of the Jews and during Christmas of the same year she worked with her nephew, Otto Frisch, on the latest ideas about the effects of neutron bombardment of uranium. Their conclusion was that the arrival of a neutron in a uranium nucleus would set up violent internal motions in the nucleus and cause it to split into two more or less equal fragments. Frisch called this fission because of its similarity to the division of a biological cell. Meitner and Frisch calculated that the nuclear reaction would lead to enormous energy being released, up to 200,000,000 electron volts, as the fission fragments flew apart. Frisch's verification of these ideas was published in the journal *Nature* in February 1939 setting 'the world of physics in an uproar'.[8] Frisch subsequently worked with Rudolph Peierls at Birmingham University producing what Per F. Dahl has described as the 'theoretical flicker', which was to lead to the breakthrough in atomic energy research.[9]

Structure of the book

The *annus mirabilis* of nuclear physics was 1939 with major discoveries taking place on the outbreak of the Second World War. This provides the starting point for the book's second chapter. The aim of the chapter is to look at a number of facilities in Wales that played a role in the early atomic energy experiments and the role of a number of Welshmen who played a critical part in events which led to the development of the first atomic weapons in 1945. Chapter 3 then looks at the major events in the UK in the post-war period which led to the decision to develop an independent British nuclear force after wartime collaboration with the United States ended, and the creation of a team of scientists and engineers that actually developed atomic and subsequently thermonuclear weapons in the 1950s and early 1960s. Having set the broader context chapter 4 goes on to look at the role played in this programme by a significant number of Welsh scientists and engineers. The chapter looks at their role in the nuclear testing programme and in the re-establishment of a close nuclear partnership with the United States from 1958 which developed further with the sale of Polaris missiles to Britain in 1963. Chapter 5 then returns to the broader context and looks at the key developments in the 1960s through to the 1990s when the UK took the decision to upgrade its nuclear force with the Polaris nuclear improvement programme and eventually decided to replace the force with a new Trident missile bought again from the United States, continuing the special nuclear relationship through to the end of the Cold War and beyond. Chapter 6 charts the contribution of a new generation of Welsh scientists and engineers to the British nuclear programme as it evolved to the present day. The book ends with a discussion of why so many Welsh scientists and engineers, amongst the best that Wales has produced, contributed in significant ways to the story of one of the greatest (and controversial) scientific events of the twentieth century.

WALES AND THE WARTIME ORIGINS OF ATOMIC ENERGY

Britain was the first state that decided it was necessary to develop an atomic weapons capability. In September 1939, two days before war broke out, the Danish physicist Niels Bohr and an American colleague, J. A. Wheeler, published a paper outlining the theory of uranium fission. Their paper highlighted the importance of the fissile isotope uranium-235, which would have to be separated from uranium-238.[1] They did not believe, however, that such separation would be possible. In March 1940, two physicists in Birmingham University, Rudolph Peierls and Otto Frisch wrote a memorandum not only showing that a lump of U-235 of just 5 kg would produce an immensely large reaction needed for an atomic explosion, but also suggesting an industrial method of separating U-235.[2] Following on from the work of Rudolf Peierls and Otto Frisch the British wartime government set up the Maud Committee consisting of six eminent scientists, to study the possibility of developing a nuclear weapon.[3] In July 1940, the committee completed its report with three main recommendations. First, it argued that it was possible to construct a uranium super bomb which was 'likely to lead to decisive results in the war'.[4] Secondly, it recommended that the work on such a bomb should be continued as the 'highest priority and on the increasing scale necessary to obtain the weapon in the shortest possible time'. And thirdly, that 'the present collaboration with America should be continued and extended especially in the region of experimental work'. The highest priority that needed to be given to the project, the report argued, was due to the fact that Germany was also working on uranium research and 'the lines on which we are now working are such as would be likely to suggest themselves to any capable physicist'.[5]

The committee accepted that it was possible that the bomb might not be produced by the time the war ended but the members believed that the prodigious explosive power of such weapons was likely to be of such military significance in the future that every effort should be made to develop them as soon as possible. The report argued that:

> Even if the war should end before the bombs are ready, the effort would not be wasted, except in the unlikely event of complete disarmament, since no nation would care to risk being caught without a weapon of such decisive possibilities.[6]

Eddie Bowen and the Tizard Mission

A copy of the report was taken to the United States in the summer of 1941 with the US still neutral and groups of scientists were, in a rather unfocused manner, working on the possibilities of the bomb. It was only after receiving the Maud Report that the US took the project more seriously, and even before Pearl Harbour, the Manhattan Project was set up.[7] By this time Britain had set up an organization with the code name 'Tube Alloys' with the aim of establishing the research and industrial programme necessary to develop atomic weapons.[8]

One Welshman, Edward ('Eddie') George Bowen, played a key role in passing on the information contained in the Frisch-Peierls Memorandum to the United States, and thereby establishing the close Anglo-American nuclear collaboration that was to follow. Eddie Bowen was the son of a sheet metal worker from Cockett, near Swansea. He joined Swansea University as a brilliant scholar at the very young age of 16 and graduated with a first-class honours degree in physics in 1930.[9] He had a masters degree in science at the age of 19 and completed his PhD at King's College, London in 1934. His research attracted the attention of R. A. Watson-Watt and he became part of his team at Orfordness working on experimental ground radar. As part of this team he made a major contribution to the development of aircraft radar, establishing himself by the outbreak of the war as one of the leading British scientists of the day. In August 1940 he was chosen to be part of a mission led by Sir Henry Tizard (and including Professor Cockcroft) to visit the United States (before they had joined the war) to pass on Britain's most important military secrets, including a sample of a cavity magnetron and details of Britain's latest uranium research.[10] Bowen was responsible for carrying the metal deed box (known as 'Tizard's Briefcase') containing all the technological secrets. When he arrived at Euston station he handed it to a porter and as he gathered up his belongings he watched the porter disappear into the crowd in search of the boat train to Liverpool. Fortunately, he was eventually re-united with the box and, following the sea voyage, delivered it, with his colleagues to the United States.

In discussions with American scientists, Tizard and Cockcroft discovered that although similar research was being undertaken in the US (especially by Enrico Fermi at Columbia University) the research was several months behind that conducted in Britain. The findings of the Maud Reports were also passed on to the US later in 1941 and played an important part in accelerating the US nuclear programme. (Bowen's work played a major part in the Battle of the Atlantic for which he was awarded the OBE in 1941 and the US Medal of Freedom in 1947. He went on to have a very distinguished scientific career in the field of radiophysics in Australia after the war.[11])

The atomic scientist: Evan James Williams

Included in the research passed on to the Americans during the Tizard Mission was information about the MDS (magnetic detection of submarines) system which had been developed by another Welsh scientist, Evan James Williams. Williams was born in 1903 in Cwmsychbant in Ceredigion. His father was a stonemason. He went to school in Llandysul and at the age of 16 won a scholarship to Swansea University where he studied physics. After obtaining a first-class honours degree in 1923, followed by a masters degree, he did research under Lawrence Bragg at Manchester University, obtaining his doctorate in 1926.

This was followed by another degree at the Cavendish Laboratory where he studied under Ernest Rutherford. His research focused on atomic collisions and sub-atomic particles, involving the impact of fast electrons on atoms. In 1933 he spent a year working with one of the greatest scientists of his day, Niels Bohr, in Copenhagen. He later went on to lecture in physics at Manchester University and Liverpool University, where he worked with James Chadwick. In 1938 at the age of 35 he was appointed to the chair of physics at Aberystwyth University and in 1939 he was elected Fellow of the Royal Society. When war broke out he joined the experimental physicist, P. M. S. Blackett, at RAE Farnborough to work on methods to stop the U-boat threat to British wartime shipping. He often discussed his work with Winston Churchill. His research, passed on to the Americans in 1940, was taken up with great enthusiasm by American scientists.

Williams was one of Wales's most distinguished atomic scientists who worked with some of the greatest scientists of his day and made a significant contribution to the Allied war effort. Sadly, his research into sub-atomic particles, and especially the meson, was cut short by his premature death at the age of 42 in September 1945. In his obituary for the Royal Society, Professor Blackett (who won the Nobel Prize for physics in 1948) described him as 'one of the most brilliant physicists' of his generation. In highlighting his major achievements, he said: 'We physicists feel constantly his loss. His distinctive gift of deep physical understanding ... would have been of the greatest value to us today.'[12]

Gaseous diffusion experiments and the contribution of the Rhydymwyn Valley Works and the Mond Nickel Company in Clydach

Following the groundbreaking insights contained in the Frisch-Peierls Memorandum and the Maud Reports, early research on extracting U-235 from uranium ore by turning it into uranium hexafluoride was undertaken in Wales. This took place in the Rhydymwyn Valley Works, near Mold in Flintshire. Leading British scientists, including Professor

James Chadwick, the Australian-born Mark Oliphant, Rudolph Peierls, his deputy Klaus Fuchs, and Otto Frisch were involved in this research.[13] Another scientist involved in the difficult early work on the gaseous diffusion process of extracting U-235 was Professor Francis Simon of the Clarendon Laboratory in Oxford University. Professor Simon worked closely with Professor Peierls and engineers from ICI and Metropolitan-Vickers to build experimental model machines which could be used in a full-scale gaseous diffusion plant. The aim was to build single-stage, two-stage and ten-stage models 'to test the pumps, the impellers and the basic membrane assembly'.[14] Because of their physical size and weight it was not possible to install these machines either in the Clarendon laboratories or at the Metropolitan-Vickers base at the Trafford Park Industrial Estate in Manchester. In early 1942 it was decided to erect the models as near to the Metropolitan-Vickers factory as possible. As a result, a disused section of a Ministry of Supply factory at the Valley Works (Pyro Building P6) was turned over for this purpose.[15]

According to Margaret Gowing, the official nuclear historian, 'The Valley models ... provided a focus for the membrane development that was crucial to the whole gaseous diffusion problem.'[16] The membranes were porous sheets through which uranium hexafluoride (a gaseous compound of uranium) was pumped. The holes had to be extraordinarily small and close together and the membrane itself very thin if the gas was to separate. The U-235 molecules would pass through the holes of the barrier faster than the U-238 molecules and there would be many stages, each yielding a slightly higher enrichment of U-235 than the preceding one. The enriched U-235 hexaflouride is later reduced to metallic uranium via an oxide reduction process.[17] Simon's specification was for holes with a diameter of 0.0001 inch and spaced at intervals of 400/450 per linear inch. And the membranes were to be only 0.001–0.002 inch thick. It was important that the membranes didn't get blocked: 'they had to be strong and remain rigid in operation, and they must be made to an extremely high standard of uniformity: the process used must be capable of mass production to very fine limits'.[18] (See Figure 1.)

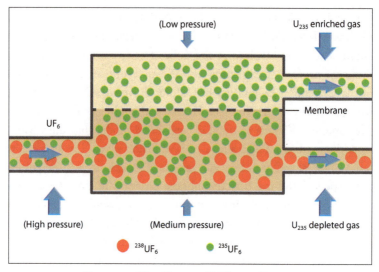

FIGURE 1 The Gaseous Diffusion Process
(by permission of Brian Burnell)

To achieve this, Professor Simon experimented with a number of different membrane materials, including wire gauze, techniques derived from engraving and lithography. In autumn 1942 a British team visited the United States specifically to study membrane development where they were introduced to the idea of membranes made from sintered nickel powder. This involved making a mesh by dissolving zinc out of an alloy with silver. The Americans were already negotiating with a British subsidiary of International Nickel, the Mond Nickel Company in Clydach, near Swansea. According to Colin Barber, 'Mond in Clydach was the only company in the world who were capable of manufacturing the nickel mesh, certainly in the volume which was required.'[19] The sintered nickel membranes from Mond were chosen for both the US and British experimental machines.

The research programme for the models at Valley was conducted under the direction of Professors Simon and Peierls. Working closely with Metropolitan-Vickers and ICI, research teams were set up at the site. In December 1941 it was estimated that the single stage and two-stage models would be ready for experiments in six to eight months (by August 1942) and the ten-stage models would arrive at intervals of six weeks thereafter. Unfortunately, performance lagged badly and continuously behind forecast. The initial experiments with the single-stage machines did not begin until New Year's day in 1943 and the first runs of two-stage machines didn't begin until August 1943. The work on the ten-stage machines did not begin at all. The manufacture of these very novel machines taxed the resources of Metropolitan-Vickers much more than expected.

Initially Britain had wanted to collaborate with the US on nuclear research but not to merge the two projects. In 1942 and early 1943, however, the US had surged ahead of Britain with its vastly superior resources and Britain looked to establish a much closer nuclear partnership. After some reluctance from the American government and a number of false starts, in 1943 the Quebec Agreement was signed between the two countries establishing a close wartime partnership on atomic energy research. After the Quebec Agreement all stocks of nickel powder of a type that was only made by the Mond Company were turned over to the United States War Department and the factory was expanded to meet American needs. This involved producing 3,000 tons of the powder that was required by the American atomic energy project.[20] At the same time British scientists and engineers (including some from the Mond Nickel Factory) joined their American counterparts on the Manhattan Project.

A Welshman at the heart of the Manhattan Project: Arthur Llewelyn Hughes

One Welshman, living in the United States, became an important part of the Manhattan Project. Arthur Llewelyn Hughes was born in Liverpool in 1883 to a Welsh-speaking family and attended a Calvinistic Methodist Welsh Chapel. His father was a coal merchant who died when he was fourteen, forcing him to leave school to help his mother. His mother subsequently moved back to her family in Abergele but Arthur stayed on to study at night school to get a place at Liverpool University, which he achieved in 1903. Initially he wanted

FIGURE 2 Arthur Llewelyn Hughes (by permission
of Washington University, St Louis, USA)

to be a teacher but he was persuaded by Charles Barkla to study physics. Barkla, an eminent physicist himself, went on to win a Nobel Prize.
Arthur obtained a degree in physics in 1906 and two years later an
MSc. On Barkla's recommendation he went on to become a research
scholar at Emmanuel College, Cambridge studying under Professor
J. J. Thompson, the Cavendish Professor of Experimental Physics and
another Nobel Laureate. He obtained a DSc from Liverpool in 1912.
While he was studying at the Cavendish he met Niels Bohr who he
kept in touch with in his later career.

On the advice of Professor J. J. Thompson, he took up a post as an
assistant professor of physics at the Rice Institute in Houston, Texas in

September 1913. In 1917, however, he returned to Britain to work for the Admiralty on anti-submarine devices. With the war over he went back to the United States and after a short spell at the Rice Institute he became the first Chown Research Professor at Queen's University in Kingston, Ontario. In 1922 he was made a Fellow of the Royal Society of Canada. Shortly afterwards he moved to Washington University, St Louis, Missouri, becoming the Crowe Professor of physics and head of the physics department. His major work on *Photoelectric Phenomena* with Lee DuBridge remained the standard text on the subject until 1959.[21]

In 1939 Hughes was asked by the Washington School of Medicine to build a cyclotron, primarily for research in nuclear medicine. This Hughes did, with the help of Dr Robert Thornton, who had worked with Dr Ernest Lawrence, who invented the cyclotron in 1930. The cyclotron was a device designed to accelerate nuclear particles by means of a strong vertical magnetic field to produce radioisotopes for study in physics, chemistry and medical research. According to one source: 'It was the most expertly engineered cyclotron of its time.'[22] It was completed in 1940 and within two years it was commandeered by the Army Manhattan Project for wartime work. Professor Arthur Holly Compton, a Nobel Prize winner and Hughes's predecessor at Washington University, was at this time director of the Metallurgical Project at the University of Chicago and worked closely with Hughes. Compton explains the importance of the Washington cyclotron in his book *Atomic Quest*:

> In order to study the chemical properties of plutonium in further detail, more and more of the material was required. At first the only source was uranium that had been exposed to the neutrons coming from one of the Berkeley cyclotrons. This cyclotron was required for other urgent experiments. Until a chain-reaction could be put into operation, another cyclotron source must be found. This was made available at Washington University in Saint Louis, where in 1940 an instrument had been built that was even better adapted to the purpose than the cyclotron at Berkeley.[23]

The Washington University cyclotron was able to run for twenty-four hours a day and to produce the then unheard of beam strength of 480 microamperes of 10 MEV deuterons. With it, the first plutonium was produced in quantities that enabled Glen Seaborg by micro-chemical means to establish the chemical properties of plutonium.' According to William Krasner:

> By the end of 1942 about 500 micrograms had been obtained – less than enough to cover the head of a pin – most of it from the Washington University cyclotron – and this was enough for the micro-chemists at Chicago to analyse successfully. On this basis the immense atomic plant at Hanford, Washington, and the eventual construction of the atomic bomb was authorized.[24]

The work of Seaborg and Enrico Fermi in converting U-238 to plutonium-239 was crucial in the wartime development of atomic weapons and Hughes's cyclotron at Washington University was an important part of this process.

The central role of Professor Arthur Holly Compton in the US atomic energy programme is worth noting. He was one of the most distinguished scientists in the US at the time. In April 1941 he was appointed by Vannevar Bush, the head of the US National Defense Research Committee (NDRC), to chair a newly appointed special committee to report on the NDRC uranium programme. Following the receipt of the Maud Report from the UK on the possibility of producing atomic weapons within a few years, the US government felt the need to review its uranium programme. Compton met with all the leading US scientists, including Ernest Lawrence, Enrico Fermi, Harold Urey, Eugene Wigner and Robert Oppenheimer, and wrote a series of reports in May and November. In these reports Compton argued that an atomic bomb could be produced before the war ended and highlighted the urgent need to speed up the US programme. In this respect his reports played the same role in the US as the Maud Reports had in the UK. As a result, Compton was put in charge of the plutonium project which many US scientists believed would be a more efficient way of producing an atomic weapon. To achieve this objective he brought together the major research groups at Columbia University, Princeton University and the University of California, Berkeley.

These groups were now concentrated at the Metallurgical Laboratory in Chicago headed by Compton. Compton's responsibility was to produce nuclear reactors to convert uranium into plutonium and to design the atomic bomb for the US. Under his leadership, Enrico Fermi built the Chicago Pile-1, which produced the first controlled nuclear chain reaction in December 1942. The Chicago laboratory was also responsible for the design and operation of the X-10 Graphite reactor at Oak Ridge, Tennessee and for the Hanford reactor. In June 1942 the Chicago laboratory became part of the Manhattan Project under the control of General Leslie Groves and Compton handed over responsibility for designing the bomb to Robert Oppenheimer at Los Alamos. Compton, however, remained a key figure in the US atomic weapons programme. In 1945 he served with Ernest Lawrence, Robert Oppenheimer and Enrico Fermi on the Special Panel that recommended to President Roosevelt the military use of the atomic bomb against Japan.[25]

The close relationship between Compton and Hughes led to Hughes himself joining the Manhattan Project in 1943. In an interview he gave in 1975 he explained that: 'one day in June 1943, Dr Louis H. Hempelmann Jr., instructor at the Mallinckrodt Institute at Washington University, came to my home with an invitation to join a highly secret war project in New Mexico'.[26] As a result he visited Los Alamos and met the director J. Robert Oppenheimer and was told that it was 'an installation where an atomic bomb was to be designed and made'. He accepted the job and returned home to pick up his belongings. He attended the wedding of his daughter and 'left the same day' to take up his post as an assistant director at Los Alamos responsible for recruiting scientists and technologists, arranging their housing and sorting out their personal problems. In June 1943 when he arrived there were 300 scientists and when he left in September 1944 there were 3,000. In this role Hughes was very much at the heart of the Manhattan Project and has been described as the project's 'father figure'. In his words:

A governing group met every Thursday at 8pm, composed of Oppenheimer, four heads of the physics, chemistry, engineering and metallurgy divisions ... and myself. If the meeting ended at 1am it was a light evening. Often we went to 3 or 4am. We would be back in work again at the normal hour.[27]

Despite playing an important part in the development of atomic weapons he was reluctant to talk about his time at Los Alamos after the war. However, he said in 1975 that: 'Seldom did I hear any discussion of whether manufacturing the bomb was the right thing to do. We were in a race with the Germans, and the Allies knew the German scientists were excellent.'[28] He also told a member of his family: 'We created a monster, but mankind in due course will benefit.'[29] ALH, as he was known, returned to his department at Washington University in 1945. Professor Arthur Holly Compton also returned to the university in 1945 after his central role in the Manhattan Project to become its chancellor. ALH later became president of the Physical Society of America. He retired in 1952 but remained very active in the university. He was described as a genial man with a good sense of humour and a fine curiosity about everything. He died in 1978 aged 94.

Conclusion

The role of Wales in these momentous events is relatively unknown. The Frisch-Peierls Memorandum was of critical importance in the development of atomic energy during the Second World War. It brought recognition for the first time that a weapon of immense explosive power could be produced before the war ended. Whoever produced that weapon first would have a decisive impact on the outcome of the war. The memorandum also highlighted the future importance of atomic energy as a source of power, as a substitute for coal and oil, in the post-war world. It led to the Maud Reports and the setting up of the Tube Alloys programme, designed to create the scientific and engineering foundations of Britain's wartime and post-war atomic energy programme. The key to that programme initially was to find a practical way to separate U-235 from U-238. Although the key breakthroughs were to be achieved in the United States, the experiments carried out at the Rhydymwn Valley Works and the nickel powder produced at the Mond Nickel Factory made a very important contribution to the wartime atomic energy programme. In their very different ways, the Welsh scientists Evan James Williams, Eddie Bowen and Arthur Llewelyn Hughes also made significant contributions – Williams to early atomic energy research, Bowen to the transfer of vital information to the United States at a critical time, and Hughes with work with the cyclotron and his involvement in the Manhattan Project.

THE BRITISH NUCLEAR PROGRAMME FROM THE 1940s TO THE 1960s

Post-war support for a British nuclear force

The contribution of Welsh scientists and engineers to the development of an independent nuclear capability in the 1940s and 1950s has to be seen in the context of the broader British nuclear programme. At the end of the war there was no doubt in the minds of many British politicians, scientists and military leaders that Britain must have its own nuclear programme.[1] In July 1945 a high level scientific committee, chaired by Sir Henry Tizard, produced a report which argued that 'the only answer … to the atomic bomb is to be prepared to use it ourselves in retaliation. A knowledge that we were prepared, in the last resort, to do this might well deter an aggressive nation.'[2] As a result, the committee argued, Britain should undertake large-scale research into atomic energy; design and manufacture of fast high-flying jet-powered bombers; and be prepared to use atomic bombs against a potential aggressor.

These ideas expressed by some of the leading scientists of the day provided the framework for the nuclear deterrent philosophy that was subsequently developed by Britain's military chiefs. In August 1945 the Admiralty followed the Tizard Report by arguing that:

> The net effect of the Atomic Bomb is that the price worth paying for peace is very much higher, and the main function of our armed forces should be the prevention of a major war, rather than the ability to fight it on purely military grounds after the war has

already been decided by the collapse of civilian morale, or the destruction of ports and industrial installations.[3]

Similar ideas were expressed by the chiefs of staff (COS) in October 1945 when they concluded that 'the possession of atomic weapons of our own would be vital to our security'. 'The best method of defence against the new weapons', they argued, 'is likely to be the deterrent effect that the possession of the means of retaliation would have on a potential aggressor'.[4] Like scientists on Tizard's committee, they urged the government to press ahead in the field of research and development in order to start the production of atomic weapons 'as soon as possible'. In response to the COS report, the government decided the same month to set up a research and experimental establishment at Harwell to undertake research on all aspects of atomic energy.

The military chiefs were particularly worried by the experience of the Blitz and the impact of the new technology given Britain's geographical location.[5] These anxieties were clearly expressed in an RAF assessment of the impact of atomic weapons on Britain's future security produced in December 1945.[6] As a small island, it was argued that Britain's cities would be highly vulnerable to attack by a relatively small number of nuclear weapons. Believing that Russia was the only likely opponent, even at this early stage in the post-war period, the RAF Future Planning Staff suggested that British security could best be achieved in the years ahead by threatening Russian cities. A similar emphasis on Britain's acute vulnerability emerged in a report by the Chiefs of Staff Joint Technical Warfare Committee in July 1946. They argued that 'some 30 to 120 atomic bombs accurately delivered by the USSR might cause the collapse of the United Kingdom without invasion'.[7]

Such beliefs, however, were not shared by everyone. Professor P. M. S. Blackett, a member of Prime Minister Attlee's Advisory Committee on Atomic Energy conducted a study of the effects of atomic weapons and Britain's vulnerability. His belief was that Britain's long-term security would be undermined rather than increased by the development of nuclear weapons. He argued that the threat to use such weapons would be counterproductive. It would be better to concentrate on the peaceful uses of atomic energy.[8] Blackett's views, however, were not accepted by other leading nuclear scientists or by the COS. Attlee agreed with other members of what can be described as a 'nuclear advocates' group (of senior scientists and military officials) who believed in the need for a nuclear deterrent strategy. In a rather dismissive response, he argued that 'the author, a distinguished scientist, speaks on political and military problems which he is a layman'.[9]

The decision to develop a British nuclear deterrent force

That the prime minister himself seemed to favour the development of atomic weapons was apparent in a number of decisions made by the Labour government in 1945 and 1946. On 10 August 1945 Attlee set up a special ad hoc committee (GEN 75) to act as 'a forum for decision-making on atomic energy policy'.[10] This was followed in January 1946 by the appointment of Lord Portal (a former air chief) as the controller of Production of Atomic Energy in the Ministry of Supply and, in August 1946, the chiefs of staff placed a requisition for an atomic bomb. By this stage, however, the government still had not made a formal decision to develop nuclear weapons.

In August 1946, despite the wartime agreements with the Americans at Quebec (1943) and Hyde Park (1944), the McMahon Act was passed in the United States, cutting off the possibility of nuclear collaboration with Britain.[11] This raised the question of whether Britain should go ahead with its own independent nuclear programme. On 19 November 1946 Portal wrote to the prime minister arguing that a formal decision by the government was required. This led to a special, highly secret, meeting of a select group of government ministers (GEN 165), which met on 8 January 1947. The committee was faced with three options: (1) not to develop atomic weapons; (2) to develop atomic weapons through the normal process through the Ministry of Supply and the Service Departments; or (3) to develop the weapons using 'special arrangements' to keep the production secret. Ernest Bevin, the foreign secretary, argued that it was vital for Britain to develop atomic weapons because 'she could not afford to acquiesce in an American monopoly of the new development'. All the ministers present agreed, supporting the third option to ensure that the production of the weapons remained secret.[12] This was also the view of the key scientists involved in work on atomic weapons. The scientist William Penney, known as 'the father of the British atomic bomb' was of the strong belief that: 'The discriminative test for a first class power is whether it has made an atomic bomb and we have either got to pass the test or suffer a serious loss of prestige both inside the country and internationally.'[13]

The official historian Margaret Gowing has argued that the decision was not the result of a perception by those involved of an immediate threat to Britain, although anxieties about the Soviet Union were growing at the time. Rather, it was the result of:

> something fundamentalist and almost instinctive – a feeling that Britain must possess so climacteric a weapon in order to deter an atomically armed enemy, a feeling that Britain as a Great Power must acquire all the major new weapons, a feeling that atomic weapons were a manifestation of the scientific and technological superiority on which Britain's strength so deficient if measured in sheer numbers of men, must depend.[14]

Apparent here are the deep-seated ideas and beliefs inherent in British strategic culture which emphasised great power status, the utility of capital weapon systems to deter threats, and the importance of staying at the leading edge of scientific and technological prowess to offset deficiencies in manpower. These were all important attributes of Britain's historic approach to national security.

The development of the British atomic capability

As the controller of production, atomic energy, Lord Portal had the task of putting together a team that would implement the government's decision in January 1947 to develop atomic weapons. To achieve this, he appointed a number of top scientists and engineers who were to be at the heart of the atomic programme. His initial appointments included the nuclear physicist and Nobel Prize winner, John Cockcroft, as director of the Atomic Energy Research Establishment based at Harwell; Christopher Hinton, a senior ICI engineer was chosen to design and construct the atomic pile, who based himself at Risley; Michael Perrin, another former ICI man, to act as his technical advisor; and Sir James Chadwick, another Nobel Prize winner and described as 'one of Britain's greatest living scientists', who also provided him with scientific advice.[15] A little later he appointed William Penney, the chief superintendent of Armament Research, who had played an influential role in the Manhattan Project, to oversee the vital work on the military applications of atomic energy. All had a firm belief in the importance of Britain developing atomic weapons.

Their task, however, was to be far from easy or straightforward. A range of industrial complexes had to be built up:

> one, to extract and refine uranium metal from ore, which was to be built at Springfields, near Preston in Lancashire; the pile itself at the Sellafield site, soon to be renamed Windscale; and a third to extract and refine plutonium which was manufactured in the course of the nuclear reaction inside the pile.[16]

Scientists and engineers had to be recruited, which proved extremely difficult in the early years after the Second World War. All of the various organisations had to be effectively coordinated. At this time only limited knowledge about how to design and develop a bomb was available from a small number of scientists and engineers who had taken part in the American Manhattan Project during the war. Brian Cathcart has summed up the range of difficulties faced by William Penney and his colleagues in the following way:

> The story of the making of Britain's first atomic bomb is one of improvisation and struggle, of hesitation and last minute rush, of high stakes and low cards ... the atomic project (was) ... characterized by a somewhat evolutionary approach to organization and by a desperate struggle for resources. The right man (William Penney)

was put in charge … but he found his path obstructed by many obstacles, from official secrecy to bureaucratic obstinacy … many mistakes were made and it was by luck as much as judgement that failure was avoided. All this confusion and haste was owed in large part to the circumstances of the country, exhausted by six years of war and groping to define its place in a changed world.[17]

Despite all the difficulties, Penney proved to be highly effective in coordinating all the complex elements of what was largely an indigenous programme. Given his previous important role in the Manhattan Project, however, he received 'a lot of stuff under the counter' from former scientific colleagues in the United States, despite the 1946 McMahon Act in the United States forbidding such cooperation.[18] This began what might be described as a 'transatlantic advocacy coalition' of UK and US scientists and engineers that were to play an important part in the British nuclear programme in the future.

The first British test of an experimental plutonium device (Operation Hurricane) took place in the Monte Bello islands off the north-west coast of Australia in October 1952.[19] In the circumstances, whatever views one holds about the morality of the project, the Hurricane test was a major success for British science and engineering.

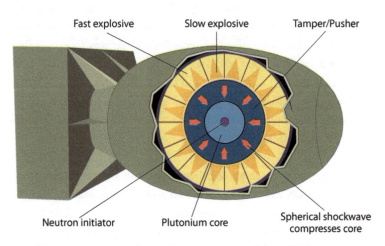

Figure 3 Atomic device (by permission of Alex Wellerstein)

Nevertheless, Britain did not, however, immediately possess an atomic weapons capability. Various technical problems still had to be overcome before an operational weapon system (Blue Danube) became available. There were also problems associated with matching weapons to aircraft, especially as the V-bombers, designed to carry Britain's atomic weapons, were not scheduled to enter service until 1955.[20]

Further tests took place in October 1953 at Emu field, south-west of Woomera in Australia (Operation Totem) with the first Blue Danube atomic bombs delivered to RAF Bomber Command's armaments school at Wittering between 7 and 14 November 1953. It was hoped to have five bombs ready by the end of 1953, with three delivered in November and a further two in December.[21] Trials to match the new weapons to the Valiant bombers which were to deliver them did not, however, begin until July 1955. The first assembly of live radioactive components of atomic weapons took place on 28 July. This date marked the moment when 'the RAF had an atomic bomb capability' for the first time (though the first live drop from an aircraft did not in fact take place until 11 October 1956 at Maralinga in South Australia).[22] Nevertheless, the RAF had an 'emergency' operational capability from mid-1955 onwards.

Another set of trials took place at Monte Bello between January and June 1956 (Operation Mosaic) and at Maralinga from July to November 1956 (Operation Buffalo). The main purpose of the Mosaic tests was to boost the yield of atomic weapons by using a layer of lithium-6 deuteride around fissile material to encourage a thermonuclear reaction. In the Buffalo series an experimental design known as 'Red Beard' was used to test the idea of a trigger, later known as a primary, to ignite a thermonuclear explosion, many times greater than the yield of atomic weapons. The tests were also designed to produce lighter smaller warheads and gain more knowledge about boosting fission warheads.

The development of thermonuclear weapons and relations with the United States

Following the American McMahon Act there was widespread belief in the UK political and military establishment that Britain remained a great power, second only to the United States and the Soviet Union. As atomic weapons were seen by many as 'the last word' in weapons, they felt Britain had to have them, and there was reluctance in government and defence circles to become overly dependent on the United States. Reflecting this view, the foreign secretary, Ernest Bevin, argued forcefully that Britain had to push ahead with its own programme 'so that it could negotiate with the US government on the basis of equality'.[23] This concern that the US should not be allowed to retain a monopoly of nuclear weapons remained an important feature of British policy in the years ahead.

Increasingly, however, it was also recognised that close collaboration in nuclear matters with the United States would be of critical importance to Britain's longer term security. Between 1948 and 1958 numerous attempts were made by both Labour and Conservative governments to repeal or amend the McMahon Act and reopen a nuclear partnership with the United States. In 1948 a modus vivendi agreement was signed, which opened up an exchange of information on medical issues relating to health and safety, extraction chemistry, natural uranium reactors and general research experience with low-power reactors. This was generally disappointing to the British, however, and following the first Soviet atomic test in August 1949, new talks took place which opened up the possibility of Britain relying on a US stockpile of atomic weapons based in the UK, while continuing its own research programme. The arrest of the atomic spy Klaus Fuchs in January 1951, however, dashed hopes of an immediate agreement. Fuchs had been at the heart of the Manhattan Project during the war and the preparations for a British nuclear force in the post-war period. The leaking of the most vital nuclear secrets to the Soviet Union was seen in the United States as a central reason for the surprise Soviet nuclear test in 1949. Closer nuclear ties with the UK were therefore opposed by many within the Truman administration fearful of more US secrets being past to the Kremlin as the Cold War was gathering momentum.

For Britain, it was believed that the only hope was to continue with its own independent programme in order to convince the US government that it had something to offer. This was becoming increasingly difficult, however, in the early 1950s as the United States (in 1952) and then the Soviet Union (in 1953) moved on to develop thermonuclear weapons just as Britain's atomic programme came to fruition with the first British test at Monte Bello on 3 October 1952. This meant that the British were effectively playing catch-up again and, from the point of view of the US, Britain did not appear to have too much to offer aside from bases for US bombers which had limited range and could not reach the Soviet Union from the US mainland. At the time, one US congressman asked about the possibility of nuclear cooperation with the British said, in rather dismissive terms, 'We would be trading a horse for a rabbit.'[24]

In 1954, however, the US government finally agreed to a limited amendment of the McMahon Act. For the Churchill government this was a significant step forward but the new US Atomic Energy Act did not open up the prospect of any American help with thermonuclear weapons. Between April and July 1954, therefore, a special H-bomb Committee (GEN 465) met to discuss whether Britain should develop its own thermonuclear weapons. In the debates that followed, three key issues were important. First, the development of such weapons was seen by some members of the government as a *sine qua non* for re-establishing much greater collaboration, at a later date with the United States. Thermonuclear weapons could help Britain achieve greater interdependence with the United States.[25] Another important factor concerned US strategic plans. At this time, there was a growing concern in both political and military circles that worrying trends in US nuclear policies might lead Britain into a war with the Soviet Union, even though Britain did not have a full understanding of US strategic plans. Even Churchill believed that:

> The danger is that the Americans may become impatient. I know their people – they may get angry and say: ... Why should we not go it alone? Why wait until Russia overtakes us? They could go to the Kremlin and say: These are our demands. Our fellows have been alerted. You must agree or we shall attack you.[26]

Only through the development of British thermonuclear weapons was it believed by some members of the GEN 465 Committee that Britain

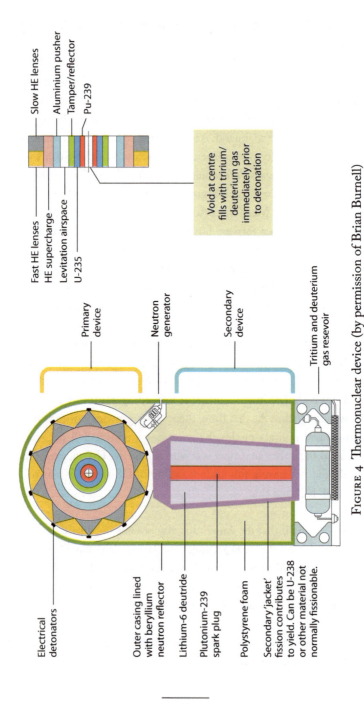

Fast HE lenses
Slow HE lenses
HE supercharge
Aluminium pusher
Levitation airspace
Tamper/reflector
U-235
Pu-239

Void at centre fills with tririum/deuterium gas immediately prior to detonation

Primary device

Neutron generator

Secondary device

Tritium and deuterium gas resevoir

Electrical detonators

Outer casing lined with beryllium neutron reflector

Lithium-6 deutride

Plutonium-239 spark plug

Polystyrene foam

Secondary 'jacket' fission contributes to yield. Can be U-238 or other material not normally fissionable.

FIGURE 4 Thermonuclear device (by permission of Brian Burnell)

could have an influence over US strategic planning.[27] The third key issue was the strong belief amongst some members of GEN 465 of the importance of a thermonuclear capability to Britain's continuing role as a great power. This was particularly the view of the prime minister. Churchill told the cabinet in July 1954 that Britain 'could not expect to maintain its influence as a world power unless it was prepared to develop the most up-to-date nuclear weapons'.[28]

This was a view strongly supported by the chiefs of staff. Sir Rhoderick McGrigor, the chief of the naval staff, argued that Britain was 'a leading world power' and had 'a position to maintain in world affairs'. He strongly believed, he said, that:

> If our influence were to decline it would be virtually impossible to regain our rightful place as a world power. It was essential that the United Kingdom should have the ability to produce the H-bomb in order that she could claim membership of the Allied H-Club.[29]

These were not, however, the only views considered by the cabinet committee. One member of the committee argued that British thermonuclear weapons would encourage further nuclear proliferation. According to this view, the wider expansion of nuclear weapons would in the longer run work against British interests. More specifically, it was argued that a decision by Britain to refrain from the development of thermonuclear weapons would have a powerful impact on West German thinking and would encourage them to abstain from developing such weapons themselves, despite their growing technological and scientific expertise.[30]

Such arguments, however, were not accepted by the committee as a whole. Most members did not believe that a British decision not to develop an H-bomb would have any impact on West Germany decisions. Nor did they accept that broader nuclear proliferation would occur as a result of a British decision in favour of such weapons. Backed strongly by the COS and leading nuclear scientists the government decided in July, therefore, to move beyond the atomic bomb programme to develop Britain's own thermonuclear weapons.[31]

TABLE I British atmospheric nuclear weapons tests
in Australia and the Pacific Ocean, 1952–8

Operation name	Round	Location	Date of firing	Yield
Hurricane		Off Trimouille Island, Monte Bello Islands, Western Australia	3 Oct. 1952	25kt
Totem	1	Emu Field, South Australia	14 Oct. 1953	10 kt
	2	Emu Field, South Australia	26 Oct. 1953	8 kt
Mosaic	1	Trimouille Island, Monte Bello Islands, Western Australia	16 May 1956	15 kt
	2	Alpha Island, Monte Bello Islands, Western Australia	19 June 1956	60 kt+
Buffalo	1	One Tree, Maralinga Range, South Australia	27 Sept 1956	15 kt
	2	Marcoo, Maralinga Range, South Australia	4 Oct. 1956	1.5 kt
	3	Kite, Maralinga Range, South Australia	11 Oct. 1956	3 kt
	4	Breakaway, Maralinga Range, South Australia	21 Oct. 1956	10 kt
Grapple	1 Short Granite	Off Malden Island, Pacific Ocean	15 May 1957	0.3 Mt*
	2 Orange Herald	Off Malden Island, Pacific Ocean	31 May 1957	0.72 Mt*
	3 Purple Granite	Off Malden Island, Pacific Ocean	19 June 1957	0.2 Mt*
Antler	1	Tadje, Maralinga Range, South Australia	14 Sept 1957	1 kt

(continued)

Operation name	Round	Location	Date of firing	Yield
	2	Biak, Maralinga Range, South Australia	25 Sept 1957	6 kt
	3	Taranaki, Maralinga Range, South Australia	9 Oct. 1957	25 kt
Grapple X		Off Christmas Island, Pacific Ocean	8 Nov. 1957	1.8 Mt*
Grapple Y		Off Christmas Island, Pacific Ocean	28 Apr. 1958	3 Mt
Grapple Z	1 Pennant	Christmas Island, Pacific Ocean	22 Aug. 1958	24 kt*
	2 Flagpole	Off Christmas Island, Pacific Ocean	2 Sept 1958	1 Mt*
	3 Halliard	Off Christmas Island, Pacific Ocean	11 Sept 1958	0.8 Mt*
	4 Burgee	Christmas Island, Pacific Ocean	23 Sept 1958	25 kt*

+ It was suggested at the Royal Commission on the Australian Tests in 1985 that the yield of this test may have been as high as 98 kilotons.

* MOD estimates made available in October 1993.

Source: The National Radiological Protection Board (NRPB 266) ICRF, Second Report, December. 1993. Reproduced by permission of Public Health England.

The Grapple tests and the Mutual Defence Agreement (MDA) with the US

These decisions led, after three years of intensive efforts, to the Grapple test series from May 1957 to September 1958 in which British scientists and weaponeers demonstrated the ability to develop boosted-fission and thermonuclear weapons. These efforts, together with the perceived growing threat to the West, caused by the Soviet Sputnik launch in October 1957, led finally to the amendment of the McMahon Act in July 1958 to fully restore Anglo-American nuclear weapons collaboration. The Agreement for Co-operation on the Uses of Atomic

Energy for Mutual Defense Purposes (MDA) allowed for the exchange of information on the production and design of nuclear warheads and the transfer of fissile material between the United States and Britain. In 1959 the agreement was amended to allow for an exchange of uranium-235 for plutonium and the procurement by Britain of component parts of nuclear weapons.[32] As such, the 1958 Agreement and the 1959 Amendment ushered in a period of nuclear interdependence which has lasted through to the present day.

At the time that the Grapple tests were taking place there were pressures on the Macmillan government, both domestically and externally, to enter into a formal agreement prohibiting nuclear tests. These early ideas to create cooperative international rules to regulate East-West hostility were later to be supported by the prime minister in the negotiations that led to the Partial Test Ban Treaty in 1963. In the late 1950s, however, it was believed to be much more important to develop Britain's own thermonuclear capability, for reasons of national security and to enhance British diplomatic interests, before such restrictions were introduced. There was a recognition of the value of moving towards a more rules-based approach to international security, but not before Britain had developed its own effective nuclear capability, in case such an approach (as was believed to be likely) proved to be ineffective.[33]

Independence and interdependence: the procurement and operation of Polaris

The important role of elite beliefs relating to 'independence' and 'interdependence' continued to reveal themselves in the years ahead. In 1960 the potential vulnerability of Britain's nuclear delivery systems, the V-bombers and the proposed Blue Streak missile system, led to a decision to purchase the air-launched Skybolt system from the United States. The subsequent US cancellation of Skybolt resulted in a crisis in Anglo-American relations. This was resolved in December 1962 at Nassau in the Bahamas when a British delegation led by Prime Minister Harold Macmillan and the United States, led by President John F.

Kennedy, came to an agreement for the sale of Polaris to the UK. And in April 1963 a detailed Polaris Sales Agreement (PSA) was signed between the two countries. The PSA became the vehicle for the transfer of Polaris technology to Britain with Britain agreeing at Nassau to commit Polaris to NATO – alongside a national right of withdrawal where supreme national interests were at stake. The 1958 MDA and 1963 Polaris Sales Agreement fundamentally altered the entire basis of British nuclear weapons policy. No longer was there a truly independent British nuclear deterrent in all its aspects as had existed prior to 1958. Instead there was a cooperative nuclear alliance with the Americans based on what Harold Macmillan liked to call 'interdependency'.[34] At the highest political levels, Harold Wilson (Macmillan's successor as prime minister in 1964) and other senior figures in the cabinet felt that possession of the nuclear deterrent brought with it international importance that could not be claimed through conventional means.

Denis Healey, the Secretary of State for Defence in the Wilson government, comments in his memoirs: 'they [the UK Polaris submarines] would give Britain more of an influence, particularly in Washington, during the coming revision of NATO strategy, because they would tend to reinforce the credibility of the American deterrent'.[35] Healey also stated that it was 'essential that we had a system which could commit the Americans if *we* used it. It was a kind of insurance policy'; an insurance policy and 'catalytic deterrent' which offered Western Europe a second centre of nuclear decision making.[36]

Moreover the Labour Party could have cancelled Polaris but chose not to (despite appearing to promise to do so in their manifesto at the 1964 general election). Despite a strong pacifist tradition within the party, the majority view within the cabinet was that Britain's nuclear capability had significant utility, in enhancing UK diplomatic and security interests. The arguments for the retention of an effective strategic nuclear capability were couched in terms of international prestige with the loss of a considerable amount of influence should the UK relinquish its deterrent and leave the French as the only nuclear weapons state in Western Europe. Deterrence ideas, however, were also important. It was pointed out that:

The military repercussions could be equally serious ... the argument turns on the question whether it is realistic to suppose that we should ever be prepared to confront the Soviet Union with the threat of unilateral United Kingdom nuclear retaliation – i.e. whether we should ever seriously wish to threaten the Russians that we would destroy, by a single-handed act of our own, a large number of major Russian cities. If we must concede that it is not impossible to foresee circumstances ... we should feel bound, once again, to react to a threat to our independence as we reacted to the summer of 1940.[37]

This evocation of the Battle of Britain once again offers a key insight into British strategic culture and the reflection of state values and norms rooted in historical experience.[38] It was noted that not only were nuclear weapons an ultimate guarantee of territorial integrity but they also provided reassurance that should America once more become 'isolationist', the UK strategic deterrent, through Polaris, could be used as a nuclear tripwire making the USSR pause before initiating an attack. Moreover it was believed that nuclear weapons gave the UK the ability to punch above its weight militarily and this could not be reclaimed through conventional means alone. By the early 1960s these 'nuclear beliefs' had become firmly embedded in the thinking of most of the national political, scientific and military elite in Britain.

Conclusion

The key reasons for the development of a British nuclear capability from the 1940s to the 1960s can be found in a number of nuclear beliefs shared by important and influential political, military and scientific figures in Britain. This nuclear belief system had a number of essential characteristics. First, it was believed by governments of both the main political parties that nuclear weapons were necessary ultimately to ensure the nation's survival as a sovereign state. Secondly, as a related belief, there was a strongly held view that nuclear weapons were needed because other adversaries or potential adversaries might develop them.

The Russians had shown this to be the case and France had developed its own nuclear force from 1960 onwards, and China similarly from 1964. Others might well follow suit. Thirdly, apart from a brief period in 1949, those who advocated an independent programme argued that nuclear weapons should be developed and retained because even the closest of allies might not come to Britain's assistance in times of crisis.[39] Fourthly, it was believed that an independent programme would serve British interests towards the United States in a number of important ways. These included: helping to influence US nuclear strategy; helping to bind the US closer to British security; providing advanced scientific and technical information to improve the British nuclear programme; and providing economic savings through cooperation. Fifthly, as the chiefs of staff themselves argued, it was believed that Britain had 'an inalienable right' to produce such weapons.[40] And sixthly, supporters shared the belief that Britain was a great power and, as such, required a nuclear capability to confirm that status. Developing atomic weapons and later thermonuclear weapons was, to use Brian Cathcart's phrase, 'a test of greatness'.[41]

4

THE ROLE OF WELSH SCIENTISTS AND ENGINEERS IN THE EARLY BRITISH NUCLEAR PROGRAMME

'People sometimes noted the especially large
number of Welshmen in the team!'[1]

The development of Britain's atomic and thermonuclear weapons in the late 1940s, 1950s and early 1960s was a major scientific and engineering achievement. With very little external help and with limited resources, British scientists and engineers solved some of the most diffi-cult scientific and engineering problems of the day. In the United States, the scientists involved in the American nuclear programme became household names (especially Oppenheimer, Teller and Kistiakowsky). In Britain, apart from William Penney and William Cook, few of those involved in Britain's nuclear programme are well known to the pub-lic. Even less well known is the fact that significant numbers of those involved initially in nuclear weapons research at Fort Halstead and then at Aldermaston were from Wales. Indeed, according to one source, there were so many Welshmen at Aldermaston that they 'could turn out a full cricket side of native Glamorganshire men'.[2] There were also a significant number of Welsh scientists in the Aldermaston rugby team! We begin by looking at a number of Welsh scientists in senior positions at the Atomic Energy Research Establishment at Harwell who did important research for the British nuclear programme.

Harwell's Welshmen

Lewis Roberts was the son of a minister in the Presbyterian Church of Wales. He was born in Cardiff but brought up in Swansea, attending Swansea Grammar School before studying chemistry at Jesus College, Oxford. Lewis Roberts was one of the pioneers of the British nuclear programme. After surviving a direct hit on his home in Swansea from a German bomb in September 1940 he completed his degree in Oxford in 1943 and registered as a postgraduate student. His research project on actinide chemistry was highly relevant to the early work on uranium isotope separation being carried out by Professor Simon in the Clarendon Laboratory at Oxford.[3] As a result he moved from Jesus College to the Clarendon Laboratory and was supervised initially by Professor Simon and later by Professor Nicholas Kurti. Despite his young age (he was twenty-one in 1943), it is clear that Roberts made an important contribution to the work being done at the Clarendon Laboratory on a method to separate uranium-235 from uranium-238. As we have seen, at the time the only method considered feasible was multiple filtration of a volatile gaseous compound UF6 through a porous metal membrane through which the lighter isotope diffused a little faster than the heavier one. A key issue was the high reactivity of UF6, resulting in corrosion and plugging of the pores in the membranes. Robert's research was concerned with the microstructure and chemical reactivity of metal and composite membranes that limited the effects of corrosion and enabled isotope separation. This work on actinide isotope separation became of increasing importance to the British bomb project, particularly as restrictions were placed on access to the US work in this area after the war. For Roberts this early work marked the start of a distinguished research career in actinide chemistry.[4]

Alongside British scientific involvement in the Manhattan Project, British scientists also worked closely with Canadian and French scientists at Chalk River in Ontario on slow neutron research, both during the war and in the immediate post-war period. Roberts was part of the team working on the chemistry of isotope separation at Chalk River. He worked closely with John Cockcroft and Bob Spence, both of whom were to become directors of the Atomic Energy Research Establishment at Harwell.[5] While he was at Chalk River he was introduced to plutonium chemistry and achieved the first separation outside the US of a minute quantity of a pure plutonium compound (25mg) extracted from a fuel rod irradiated in an experimental pile assembly. At the time there was an accidental spill in his laboratory of the solution containing all of the separated plutonium that had been obtained. Armed with a sharp knife, rubber gloves and a bottle of nitric acid, he cut the linoleum containing the spill, dissolved it in nitric acid and eventually recovered almost all the plutonium!

Roberts joined the staff at Harwell in 1947 as a scientific officer in the Chemistry Division just at the time the decision was being made by the Attlee government to develop an independent nuclear deterrent. The early work at Harwell in 1947 and 1948 involved building two graphite-moderated reactors, GLEEP (the Graphite Low Energy Experimental Pile) and BEPO (the British Experimental Pile). Roberts's first task on joining Harwell's Chemistry Division was to undertake a detailed study of the microstructure and chemical reactivity of graphite by examining the pore structure of synthetic graphite. By using liquid density measurements he was able to show that a significant fraction of the pores were closed to external liquid and gaseous media. This work made a significant contribution to the UK graphite reactor programme.

Given the central importance of actinide oxides (particularly UO_2 and PuO_2) as fuel materials for fission reactors, Roberts's research quickly established his reputation as a leading scientist in this field. He was in great demand at international conferences and delivered papers at the UN International Conference at Geneva on the Peaceful Uses of Atomic Energy and at the International Atomic Energy Agency in the late 1950s and early 1960s. He later went on to have a successful career in senior management at Harwell, first as assistant director and then as deputy director at a time when the organisation's future was being questioned.[6] Roberts very successfully ran the non-nuclear diversification programme and helped to move the organisation in a more commercial direction. In 1975 he became director of Harwell, serving with great distinction until 1986 (the second longest director after Sir John

Cockcroft). During this period he adopted the lead responsibility for the difficult area of radioactive waste management, setting up NIREX (the Nuclear Industry Radioactive Waste Executive), as well as continuing with the programme of commercialisation (through the Trading Fund).

Following his retirement in 1986, his long experience with nuclear energy issues led to his appointment to the new Wolfson Chair of Environmental Risk Assessment at the University of East Anglia (UEA). In this new role he set up the Environmental Risk Assessment Unit (ERAU) which became the focus for coordinating related interests across the School of Environmental Science and other research centres, including the Climate Change Unit. The ERAU also became a collaborating centre of the World Health Organisation. After his retirement from UEA in 1990 he continued to publish on nuclear energy and environmental matters and played a role as a specialist adviser to the Secretary of State for Wales (on environmental contamination matters) and a specialist advisor to the House of Commons Defence Committee (on matters such as the decommissioning of nuclear submarines, radiation protection for civilians and the nuclear testing programme in the 1950s). Roberts, described as 'a rather shy and reserved man with a strong sense of public responsibility', died at the age of 90 in April 2012.[7]

Brian Flowers was born in Blackburn but went to Bishop Gore Grammar School in Swansea. He was also the son of a minister. He was 'a brilliant scholar' at Gonville and Caius College, Cambridge, where he obtained an MA in physics. Like Roberts, Brian Flowers joined the Anglo-Canadian Atomic Energy Project at Chalk River in 1944 at the age of just twenty. He stayed until 1946 when he was recruited by James Chadwick to AERE Harwell. He continued his research on nuclear physics until 1950 when he joined the Department of Mathematical Physics at Birmingham University to do doctoral research under Professor Rudolph Peierls. After completing his DSc in 1952 (in just two years) he returned to Harwell at the age of 28 to take over as head of the Theoretical Physics Division following the arrest of Klaus Fuchs on charges of spying for the Soviet Union. As noted earlier, Fuchs had been a key member of the Manhattan Project. He had worked closely with Professor Peierls, and as head of Theoretical Physics at Harwell he had intimate knowledge of both the British and US atomic energy projects, including early American work on the 'super' bomb (which came to fruition with the US thermonuclear tests in 1952).

During the period Flowers was at Harwell, Britain tested both atomic weapons and thermonuclear weapons and developed a series of nuclear facilities to produce the materials for the weapons and civil nuclear programmes (including the GLEEP, BEPO and Zephyr atomic piles). His research focused on quantum mechanics, the fundamental movement of small particles of energy, focusing on the structure of the atomic nucleus and nuclear reactions. These were areas in which he quickly established an international reputation. In 1958 he left Harwell to take up an academic career, first as Professor of Theoretical Physics at Manchester and later rector of Imperial College of Science and Technology. From 1985 to 1990 he was vice-chancellor of the University of London. He chaired the Science Research Council between 1967 and 1973 and the Committee of Vice Chancellors and Principles between 1983 and 1985. He also produced the Flowers Report on nuclear energy and the environment for the Royal Commission in 1976, which had a significant impact on the future development of the UK civil nuclear programme. He was knighted in 1969 and became Baron Flowers of Queensway in 1979. He was a particularly talented musician, playing both the piano and cello, and a keen angler. He died in 2010.

Walter Marshall followed fellow Welshman Brian Flowers as Head of Theoretical Physics at Harwell. He was born in Rumney in Cardiff in 1932 and attended St Illtyd's College before following Flowers to study mathematical physics at Birmingham University. He obtained a first-class degree and went on to do his PhD in two years under Professor Peierls. His thesis was on 'Antiferromagnetism and neutron scattering from ferromagnets'. At the age of 22 he joined the Theoretical Physics Division at AERE Harwell in 1954 and six years later he succeeded Brian Flowers as head of that division. By this stage he had established himself as one of the leading theoreticians in the atomic properties of matter. According to Fishlock and Roberts in a biographical memoir for the Royal Society his:

main personal contribution to the theory of the solid state related to magnetic properties, ranging from the very mathematical in discussing the statistical mechanics of magnetic phase transitions, and, in particular their critical properties, to much more phenomenological treatments of the molecular orbitals in magnetic salts, and to the theory of magnetism in transition metals, in particular alloys. He became convinced of the value of neutron scattering. Here again, his main but not exclusive interest was in magnetic substances, where he encouraged experiments on the inelastic scattering from spin waves, on the magnetic structure factors around impurities ...[8]

Fishlock and Roberts go on to argue that his main impact arose from his strong interaction with experimentalists and the driving through of programmes to test and expand theoretical understanding of real materials. In 1964 he was the recipient of the Maxwell Medal for outstanding contributions to theoretical physics from the Institute of Physics. He went on to become director of AERE in 1968, overseeing a period of great change and diversification at Harwell. He stayed in this position until 1981 when he was appointed chairman of the United Kingdom Atomic Energy Authority.

In 1983 he became chairman of the Central Electricity Generating Board. Following the government's plans to privatise electricity generation in 1989 he was made chairman of National Power. He was awarded a CBE in 1973 and he was knighted in 1983. As a result of his work in 'keeping the lights on' during the miners' strike between 1984 and 1985 he was made a life peer by Margaret Thatcher, becoming Baron Marshall of Goring in 1985. He is described as 'a person of considerable and unforgettable presence, and of many parts, a polymath and much more'.[9]

Other very bright young Welsh scientists who joined Harwell included **Dr John Lewis,** who became head of the Industrial Chemical Group and had key responsibilities for the treatment and disposal of radioactive wastes.[10] John Lewis was a contemporary of Lewis Roberts at school and they met up again at Harwell and shared similar interests in research on the disposal of radioactive waste materials.

The Welsh contingent at Fort Halstead and Aldermaston

In developing the atomic bomb, Penney's team consisted of metallurgists, physicists and chemists. Welsh scientists and engineers played an important role in all three of these areas.

The Metallurgists

Graham Hopkin was from Swansea. He trained as a metallurgist, graduating from Cardiff University. 'Hoppy' as he was known was 'a genial modest Welshman, with an engaging and out-going personality', who joined the Armaments Research Department at Woolwich in 1930 at the age of 21. He was recruited by Penney to be a part of the multidisciplinary team to work on the atomic bomb in 1947. His job was to oversee the production of the inner components of the bomb. On joining the team he was immediately faced with an entirely new range of metallurgical problems and materials, beginning with the largely unknown plutonium and going on to many more exotic and equally unpleasant substances.[11] Hopkin led the metallurgy team at Aldermaston, initially with responsibility for developing the plutonium core of the bomb, made up of two separate spheres. He and his team had to work at the forefront of what was known at the time, not only about plutonium and uranium, but also other highly dangerous materials such as polonium, beryllium and lithium deuteride. Polonium and beryllium were used to form the 'initiator', or 'Urchin', which sat at the core of the bomb assembly, designed to start the chain reaction of the fissile material. Brian Cathcart has described the role of the Urchin in the following terms:

> a tiny quantity of polonium, a metal so radioactive that it glows blue in the dark, is wrapped in the stable element beryllium … at the moment of detonation, when the convergent waves crush the core, the two metals in the 'Urchin' mix. Polonium emits a constant spray of alpha particles, and when these strike beryllium they shatter the beryllium nuclei, releasing a further spray, this time of neutrons. When these neutrons burst into the plutonium they

ignite the fission chain reaction. The trick of the initiator, then, is to provide a barrier between the two metals which separates them until the required moment, but when disrupted, unleashes the shower of neutrons.[12]

Margaret Gowing, the official historian of the British atomic energy programme, has argued that there were two special difficulties in the plutonium work that Hopkin and his staff had to deal with prior to the first British test in 1952. The first 'was to safeguard the workers from the great hazards of the material. Work on it was impossible without the highly protected hot laboratories, but even there, handling times had to be kept very short because of the radiation danger.' The second danger

was the possibility of reaching a supercritical mass in the experimental and development work. The only available nuclear constants for plutonium were those brought back from Los Alamos; they were so simple that they were not universally valid, and so it was uncertain whether they could be trusted when the system was moderated by the hydrogen and/or carbon contained in the conventional explosives which surrounded the plutonium in the bomb.

When the first plutonium casting was made at Aldermaston by Hopkin and his team shortly prior to the test in the middle of the night, they had quite a scare. As 'the metal was being melted in an argon atmosphere in a cerium sulphide crucible a ghostly blue flame appeared'. This led the team to fear that the criticality calculations were incorrect. This led one member of the team to say: 'Well boys, it's too late to run!' In fact the flame was caused by a chemical reaction due to an impurity and they were able to continue with their work.[13]

Hopkin's work was of crucial importance, not only in the 1952 Hurricane test but also in the subsequent tests from 1953 to 1958, which led to the development and deployment of British atomic weapons, boosted fission megaton weapons and thermonuclear weapons. As chief of materials he was responsible for building up the British stockpile of nuclear weapons in the 1950s. He also worked very closely with the

American scientists and played an important part in helping to re-open nuclear collaboration with the US after the McMahon Act was finally repealed with the Mutual Defence Agreement (MDA) in 1958.[14] This was described by the prime minister, Harold Macmillan, as 'the Great Prize'.[15] In the meetings following the MDA, US and British scientists, including Hopkin, worked closely together exchanging a wide range of highly secret information about each other's nuclear programmes. Hopkin was part of the team that met their American counterparts at Aldermaston and went on trips to the Los Alamos, Livermore and Sandia laboratories between December 1958 and February 1959. These visits laid the foundations for the Joint Working Groups (JOWOGs) of scientists from which the British nuclear programme benefitted enormously. The mutual respect between the scientists involved was of crucial importance in the 'special nuclear partnership' that emerged in the late 1950s and early 1960s and which lasts down to the present day. Hopkin and his staff have been described as being among 'the heroes of the British H-Bomb story'.[16] He became deputy director of Aldermaston in 1965 and was appointed CBE in 1967 for his 'outstanding contribution to scientific research and development'. He was a keen golfer, squash player and fisherman. He retired in 1973.

Geoffrey Ellis was born in Ammanford and graduated from Swansea University. Like Hopkin, Ellis did important work in the metallurgy field, developing the intricate techniques required to prepare and machine beryllium to the required shape, a highly dangerous light metal used in the initiator of the bomb. The dust from beryllium can cause a lung disease very similar to pneumoconiosis. Very little was known in Britain about beryllium at the time. Fortunately, it could be purchased from the United States without breaching the stringent terms of the McMahon Act. Ellis was highly respected by other members of the metallurgy team and later became involved in many of the JOWOGs set up after the 1958 MDA with the United States. He went on to become head of metallurgy at Aldermaston in the 1970s and 1980s and played a central role in the production of nuclear warheads during the Polaris Improvement Programme. It is also said that he was known at Aldermaston as being a very good squash player![17]

Colin Hughes was a miner's son from Cefn Fforest, near Blackwood. Hughes also played an important role in the metallurgy team helping to produce the plutonium core for the Hurricane test and inserting it into the bomb in October 1952. The problem that Hughes and his colleagues faced was that plutonium was to be made in the reactors at Windscale but this would not be available before the early part of 1952. Some experimental plutonium was delivered from Chalk River in 1951 but, apart from this, the team had to rely on snippets of information leaked from the United States prior to the plutonium arriving from Windscale. Apart from the Hurricane test, Hughes was also subsequently involved in the Totem test at Emu Field in the Australian desert.

The Physicists
Amongst the Welsh physicists involved in the early British nuclear programme **Ieuan Maddock** was perhaps the most interesting. He was a miner's son from Gorseinon who attended Gowerton County Grammar School. He left school believing he was destined to become a carpenter but he went on to Swansea University where he obtained a first-class degree in physics, before going on to PhD research on optical measurement. He was a small, intense man with a balding pate and a moustache who had a native genius for electronic instrumentation. He is said to have made an outstanding contribution to the bomb programme with his work on the design and development of electronic instrumentation and telemetry.

William (later Lord) Penney had been given the task of building the British bomb in 1947 and he recruited Maddock, who was barely thirty years old, to his High Explosives Research (HER) team at Fort Halstead in Kent (prior to the development of Aldermaston in the early 1950s).[18] Penney had been part of the wartime Manhattan Project and had flown in the observer plane in the Nagasaki attack (with another member of the British team, Group Captain Cheshire, VC). He had also been present at the post-war US Bikini tests. He knew that one of the critical requirements of the British programme would be 'to measure the implosion time of the bomb, to monitor the firing circuit performance

FIGURE 5   Ieuan Maddock (by permission of The Royal Society)

and to measure the multiplication rate of the gamma output'. In addition, it would be necessary 'to ensure accurate timing and recording of the actual firing, to visually record events with high-speed cameras and to monitor the behaviour of all associated equipment, including such items as control and safety clocks, batteries and generators, etc.'[19]

Penney recognised Maddock's 'lively imagination and quick mind' and put him in charge of the Telemetry and Communications Division, developing the wide range of complex instrumentation needed to meet these exacting requirements.[20] In particular, he designed and developed oscilloscopes which were at the cutting edge of what was available at the time. At the critical Hurricane test in October 1952, 'the busiest team was the telemetry and communications group, responsible for the electronic firing system and for the network of communications and controls' linking the bomb and all the many field sites.[21] Maddock was the inspiring leader of the team which provided the key measurements which were an essential part of the work, not only for Hurricane, but also later tests (including the Totem, Mosaic and Buffalo series). He was also put in charge of the countdown to the detonation, earning him the nickname 'The Count of Monte Bello'. Over a ten-year period he has been described as a key 'lynchpin in British atomic weapons development'.[22] He became deputy director of Aldermaston and obtained an OBE in 1953.

Maddock later went on to do important work in the field of seismology which made a significant contribution to the Partial Test Ban Agreement between Britain, the United States and the Soviet Union in 1963. This was the agreement which banned nuclear testing in the atmosphere. He went on to work in the Ministry of Technology in 1965. He later became the chief scientist in the Department of Trade and Industry, before becoming principal of St Edmund Hall at Oxford University. He was appointed Fellow of the Royal Society in 1967, CBE in 1968 and he was knighted in 1975.

Another Welshman, **David Barnes,** a health physicist, was given the vital job at Aldermaston of protecting staff against exposure to radiation and monitoring the atmosphere for contamination. Plutonium is a highly toxic material and it was known that serious accidents had happened at Los Alamos. Barnes, tall, smartly dressed and mild of temperament, was given the important task of establishing a Health Physics Regime. This involved designing and producing a wide range of equipment and laying down safety procedures for staff at Aldermaston and those involved in the test series.[23] Barnes, like Maddock, was part of a High Explosive Research (HER) contingent sent out to the Monte Bello Islands for the Hurricane test. Halfway between Ceylon and Singapore two of the four engines of the aircraft he was travelling in gave out. The plane had to drop down to a lower altitude to continue, only to be met by a typhoon more than a hundred miles from its destination. Eventually the plane limped into the Changi airbase in Singapore, landing on a runway lined with fire engines and ambulances![24]

Aubrey Thomas was another Welshman who made his mark first in the Armament Research Establishment (ARE) in Woolwich during the Second World War and from 1952 at Aldermaston. Thomas worked in the area of X-radiography, with critical assemblies. He was an excellent physicist and mathematician who contributed to the AWE programme but who preferred not to get too far from the frontier where the real work was being done. He was one of the few scientists who really understood how to deal with experimental error. His two greatest achievements while working at Aldermaston over a 45-year period were to help his fellow Welshman, David Barnes, in the development of the world's first electron synchrotron and to show that the Hurricane atomic device was safe to assemble in 1952. This later work led to the setting up of the AWRE Criticality Panel of which he became a leading member.

Throughout his life he thought of himself as a Welsh expatriate and given half an hour with another Welshman would find that they were related! On his retirement in July 1988 he was given a book of Welsh poetry and his ruler that he had used for the past twenty years.

Four more Welsh physicists played a part in the early British nuclear programme. These were Gerald Davies, J. D. Davies, Reg Owen and Bill Rees. **Gerald Davies** obtained an MSc from Swansea University and went on to work at Farnborough in the field of magnetic amplifiers. He then went on to do a period as a science master before joining Aldermaston in 1957, working in the field of theoretical modelling and practical aspects of electrical energy transducers. In the late 1960s and early 1970s he switched to work on infrared discrimination and the effects of nuclear environments.

J. D. Davies was another Welsh scientist who worked at Fort Halstead in the early days of the atomic bomb programme. He worked in the area of weapon warhead electronic design. He attended the test trials at Maralinga and Christmas Island as the warhead firing team leader. He went on to become head of the Safety Division in 1974 and later the board member for safety. He played a key part in the reforms at Aldermaston following the Pochin Enquiry in late 1978. The enquiry looked into radiological health and safety at the establishment following the discovery that twelve workers appeared to have accumulated plutonium in their lungs in excess of the level recommended by the International Commission on Radiological Protection. The enquiry led to three active areas of Aldermaston being closed for three years.

Reg Owen was another physicist who contributed to the programme. He was born in Swansea and went to university in Aberystwyth. In 1937 he joined the Ministry of Supply and worked at Foulness as a range safety officer. He went on to work in the Research Department of the War Office at the Woolwich Arsenal and from there to HER and later Aldermaston. He was very keen on rugby and fast motorcycles. **Bill Rees** was another who worked on explosives in the war as part of an evacuated group from the Woolwich Research Department in Swansea University. He went on after the war to do explosives research at Fort Halstead as part of Penney's initial atomic weapons team.

The Chemists

Alongside the physicists and metallurgists there were a number of Welsh chemists who made a significant contribution to the early nuclear weapons programme. **David Lewis**, or 'Dai Trit', as he was known, was also the son of a miner. He was brought up in Brynmawr, and did his first degree and PhD in chemistry at Aberystwyth University. Following the completion of his PhD at Aberystwyth in 1933, he taught for four years at Quakers' Yard Secondary School. He then lectured at Cardiff University until the outbreak of war when he held various research posts before joining the Ministry of Supply's Armaments Research Establishment, first in Woolwich and then at Pembrey in Wales. After the war he joined the Research Department at Woolwich and was subsequently recruited when he was in his early forties as a member of Penney's Aldermaston team. As the superintendent of the Chemistry Division, he was responsible for helping to solve many of the complex chemical problems involved in dealing with materials at the heart of both atomic and thermonuclear weapons. Lewis has been described as 'a big burly man and a natural rugby forward'.[25] Penney considered him to be 'the second cleverest man at Aldermaston'.[26] (The first cleverest was the mathematician, John Corner.) Penney also said that he worked harder and faster than any other chemist in the establishment and his staff were inspired by his example.

In an article, written for the AWRE newsletter entitled *The Early Years: Recollections*, Lewis recalled the excitement and motivation of young scientists working on the bomb project in the period from 1947 to 1952. In his words:

> We were all relatively young and enthusiastic in those wonderful days: the newer advances of science enthralled our minds and satisfied the intellect. We worked untiringly and unceasingly on this defensive project because we had recently lived through a period when we had seen defenceless nations crushed and humiliated … It was an experience none of us will ever forget.

In his recollections of the preparations for the Hurricane test he emphasised that there were 'dangers, delays, difficulties and failures' but 'ultimately hard-won success'.[27]

Lewis was an expert on tritides or tritium gas (earning him the nickname 'Dai Trit'), which became important in the Mosaic, Buffalo and Grapple tests designed to boost the yield of Britain's weapons.[28] As we have seen, in 1954 the Churchill government decided to develop thermonuclear weapons (after similar developments in the US in 1952 and the USSR in 1953). Lewis and his colleagues played an important part in the tests held in Australia and at Christmas Island in the Pacific. In particular, he played a leading part in helping to solve formidable chemical problems associated with the corrosive reaction of tritium gas and plutonium. This involved designing and manufacturing a mechanism for inserting gas into the bomb's core just before firing. He made a particularly critical contribution to the 'Burgee' shot in the Grapple Z tests in September 1957. According to Lorna Arnold, the official historian of the British H-bomb programme

> Burgee was a very exploratory device and exceptionally difficult to handle. Designing and making it had been a formidable chemical engineering task because of the incompatibility problems with tritium and plutonium. It was difficult to contain and control highly reactive tritium gas at high pressure, and to design and manufacture a mechanism for inserting gas into the core just before firing.[29]

Lewis and his team were responsible for developing a new gas generator device (known as 'Daffodil') which helped to resolve this problem. This was an essential development in the eventual success of the test on 23 September 1957. This success helped Britain to successfully develop a gas-boosted megaton weapon, as well as a thermonuclear ('double bomb') device during the Grapple tests.[30]

Lewis later became the government chemist and in 1970 he was elected honorary Professorial Fellow of Chemistry in his old university in Aberystwyth. Interestingly, as the result of his research he discovered, he believed, two sub-atomic particles, which he christened with the Welsh terms, *tamaid* and *bach*, meaning respectively 'morsel' and 'small'.[31] Unfortunately, even though they became the subject of research, the names never caught on. Showing his versatility, in 1964 he also published a volume of Romantic poems under the title *Mountain Harvest*. Lewis missed out on a knighthood which he had been led to expect because the Wilson government in the 1960s decided to cut down on civil service honours.

Percy White was another member of the small group of highly talented scientists who were involved in the British nuclear weapons programme in the late 1940s and 1950s. He was the son of a tent-maker and seamstress who was born in London, but grew up in Swansea. He received a scholarship to his local university and graduated with first-class honours in chemistry at the age of 19. He then received a further scholarship and went to University College, London where he gained a diploma in chemical engineering. He worked initially in the metals industry in the 1930s and then went on to design power station equipment. With the outbreak of the war he joined the Ministry of Supply as a government scientist, initially working on the antidotes to chemical warfare agents. He later worked for the Royal Ordnance Factories where he made an important contribution to the war effort by developing a new method of filling shells and bombs with high explosive. After the war he worked at Waltham Abbey, in high explosive research before joining the staff at Porton Down (in the Microbiological Research Department). He then moved on to the Woolwich Arsenal, part of the Armament Research Department, headed by William Penney. Penney recruited White to the super-secret HER group in 1949 as part of an initial team of thirty-seven charged with developing Britain's atomic bomb.

When the HER group moved to Aldermaston in 1950 White was the first scientist on the site where his initial job was to research, design and commission a radioactive liquid treatment plant to produce some of the exotic materials required for the bomb project. Lorna Arnold has argued that White 'played a key role in developing Britain's first atomic bomb' and subsequently 'contributed even more significantly to the development of British thermonuclear weapons'.[32] In the early 1950s he worked in the Materials Division under Graham Hopkin before being appointed to the post of Superintendent Chemical Engineering in the late 1950s. He later became Senior Superintendent Chemical Technology. Following the Grapple tests in 1957/8 and the MDA with the United States, White, like Hopkin and other Welsh scientists, was heavily involved in the technical collaboration with American scientists which was of crucial importance in laying the foundations of the Anglo-American nuclear relationship.

Later in the 1960s he 'led a team of chemists, metallurgists and engineers doing research on the "fast-reactor" at Dounreay in Caithness', which tested nuclear materials and contributed power to the National Grid. William Penney described him as 'a highly talented engineer who was energetic and self-confident, with an enquiring mind and the ability to express himself with extraordinary clarity'.[33] After his retirement White worked as a consultant to the UK Atomic Energy Authority and to the Department of Health, making important contributions to hospital design. He was also a talented artist enameller contributing to annual exhibitions in London and holding a one-man exhibition at the Winchester City Art Gallery. He was awarded the OBE in 1966 and he died in 2013, aged 96.

Other Welsh chemists also played an important role in their respective fields. **Reg Figgins** was one who made an early contribution. He started work in the Research Department at the Woolwich Arsenal in 1938 before joining the team doing explosives research at Swansea during the war. Afterwards he also joined the HER project before joining Aldermaston in 1954 where he was responsible for setting up the Initiator Facility. His main interests were music, sailing and photography.

Given serious shortages of scientific civil servants at Aldermaston in the early 1950s there was a recruitment drive which visited a number of Welsh universities. As a result a number of talented young Welsh academic scientists, attracted by the scientific challenges associated with working at the cutting edge of their fields, joined the programme, swelling the ranks of 'taffy's boys'. David Lewis was involved in this recruitment process and one of those who joined the staff at Aldermaston as a result was **Alun Price** from Gwaun Cae Gurwen (the birthplace of Gareth Edwards, Sian Phillips and Barry Morgan, a former archbishop of Wales). Like Maddock, Lewis and Hughes, Price was the son of a miner. He attended Pontardawe Secondary School and went on to do chemistry at Aberystwyth University where he also got his PhD. He was recruited by David Lewis to work on tritium. He joined the chemistry team at Aldermaston in 1954 at an important time. The use of lithium 6 as a source of tritium had been recognised by William Penney in 1953 and a programme was initiated at Harwell, and later at Capenhurst, to separate lithium 6 from lithium metal, under the code name Project Crystal. When irradiated by neutrons lithium 6 produces tritium, which under conditions of intense pressure combines with deuterium to produce an enhanced nuclear explosion.

Just at the time that Price joined the staff at Aldermaston work was being undertaken to experiment with boosted fission weapons as the first stage of the thermonuclear programme. According to one source:

> The high pressure and temperature environment at the centre of an exploding fission weapon compresses and heats a mixture of tritium and deuterium gas (heavy isotopes of hydrogen). The hydrogen fuses to form helium and free neutrons. The energy release from this fusion reaction is relatively negligible, but each neutron starts a new fission chain reaction, speeding up the fission and greatly reduces the amount of fissile material that would otherwise be wasted when expansion of the fissile material stops

the chain reaction. Boosting can more than double the weapons fission energy release.[34]

The tritium-deuterium fusion reaction was of critical importance in the Mosaic tests and in the Grapple tests in 1957/8 which produced Britain's first thermonuclear bomb. Alun Price's work at Aldermaston in the mid-to-late 1950s contributed to this programme. He was a keen rugby and cricket player, and a good athlete. He later returned to Aberystwyth University to continue his work in the Chemistry Department.

Not all Welsh scientists who joined the staff at Aldermaston were happy there. **John Meurig Thomas** was born in 1932 in the village of Ponthenri in the Gwendraeth valley, Carmarthenshire. His father and one brother were miners. He went to Llechfedach Primary School and Gwendraeth Valley Grammar School before studying chemistry at Swansea University. He graduated with a first in 1954 and obtained his PhD in October 1957 (which was completed at Queen Mary College, London). He then joined the staff at Aldermaston as part of the chemistry team. He later described this decision as a 'stupid mistake'. He was under the impression that he 'would be trained to pursue studies in electron diffraction' but on arriving at Aldermaston he was given 'a dismal task involving electrodepositing thin films of metal on uranium'.[35] In an interview in 2007 he told Alan Macfarlane that he had been struck by the idea that 'the equipment side of Aldermaston was so good that I would enjoy myself there'. However, even after a few weeks he realised that 'this was the wrong place to be'. He said that he was 'ambivalent at best about atomic weapons and didn't want to be there'.[36] It was, however, at Aldermaston that he discovered dislocation theory which was of critical importance to his later research in solid-state chemistry. After leaving Aldermaston he was appointed to a post in Bangor University before taking up the chair in chemistry at Aberystwyth in 1964. In 1977 he was made a Fellow of the Royal Society and was appointed to the Chair of Physical Chemistry at Cambridge. In 1986 he became the director of the Royal Institution and, after being knighted in 1991, he became master of Peterhouse College in Cambridge from 1993 to

2002. His work on heterogeneous catalysis made him one of the most distinguished scientists of his day.

Other Welsh contributions to the early nuclear programme

Important work on the physical properties of liquids was also undertaken at Aldermaston by an English academic, **Neville Temperley,** in the late 1950s and early 1960s. Temperley went on to become an honorary Welshman through his work as Professor of Applied Mathematics at Swansea University from 1965 to 1982.

Significantly, a number of Welsh universities also provided research support to Aldermaston at various times during the programme in the 1950s. As an example, physicists at Swansea University played an important role just before the first Hurricane test in 1952, providing advice on how to resolve a problem with the switch (the trigatron) that sent the current to the detonators of the bomb. There was a danger of premature firing of the weapon and consultation with Swansea University scientists helped to resolve the problem. The answer they provided was to submit the trigatron to a special procedure between firings. Professors **Frank Llewelyn Jones** and **Colyn Grey Morgan,** in particular, helped with this task.[37]

The Welsh connection with nuclear weapons was not, however, confined to the work of Welsh scientists and engineers in the 1950s. Prior to Aldermaston being chosen as the main site for designing and developing atomic weapons, a site near Fairwood Common, outside Swansea was also considered. Harlech was also considered for a time as a place to build a production pile to produce plutonium. It was rejected, however, on the grounds that the Welsh would resent the desecration of so historic an area.

A Welsh scientist and the Windscale fire of October 1957

Morlais John Harris was the son of a coalminer in the south Wales valleys. In 1953, he went to Birmingham University to study physics and soon after he graduated in 1956 he joined the Atomic Energy Authority to work as a scientific officer at the Windscale plant, responsible for the production of weapons-grade plutonium.[38] He saw this appointment as a very exciting opportunity. In his words:

> There was a tremendous feeling that we were in a brand new, thriving, expanding industry. I remember someone coming into the coffee bar and saying how young we all were. There was money in this industry, people were going off to international conferences ... it was going somewhere.[39]

Morlais also found romance on the tennis courts at Windscale and married Elizabeth Tonkin, the youngest daughter of Jim Tonkin, a research chemist at the plant.

Eighteen months after joining the staff, as Windscale's work on the bomb programme continued at a breathless pace, a major incident occurred. In October 1957, one of Windscale's two 'piles' – the reactors in which the production of plutonium began – caught fire.

> Air that was pumped through the reactor as a coolant was filled with radioactive debris, which escaped through the reactor's chimney and fell on the local countryside. By the time the fire was discovered – on Thursday October 10 – it had been blazing for around 50 hours.[40]

Morlais Harris describes the incident in the following terms:

> A bus used to take us to the plant at 8.30 in the morning. I got on the bus, and somebody said, 'Hey, look at that.' Coming out of the top of the chimney was a fine, feathery little drift of pale smoke. Somebody came on board and said, 'Don't panic – go straight inside, shut the doors and windows, and don't come out until you have heard the all-clear. There's an incident at the reactor.' No work was done that morning. Very quickly, we knew it was on fire.

Morlais Harris was later summoned from his home at around 6 p.m. and driven to the plant. By that time, they needed people whose low exposure to radioactivity meant that they could put in shifts close to the reactor. As a result he was told to climb up to the top of its protective concrete cap and he spent the night taking readings from thermocouples – temperature sensors, in essence – wired into the machinery below.

Again in his words:

> I sat at a little table next to a big bank of instruments. I had sheets of graph paper and I had to take readings every now and again. I had a telephone as well. And I was told that if the reading went unstable, as if it didn't know what temperature it was recording, I had to phone up and tell them: 'Thermocouple 23 has gone on open circuit.' That meant the thermocouple had burned out. And I now know what that meant: the fire had spread. I came down the next morning at 10 o'clock and large areas of the building, inside and outside – even the grass verges and roadways – had been roped off. I now know that was because they were radioactive. They had put the fire out, eventually, by pumping water in the reactor. And they didn't know where the hell the water was going to come out. It wasn't built for that. And radioactive water came out all over the bloody place.

There was a very serious issue involved in putting out the fire with water. By adding water to the molten metal in the reactor it could easily have caused a catastrophic, Chernobyl-type explosion. Nobody quite knew what the outcome would be. 'At the time, I wasn't anxious at all,' he later claimed. 'I was 21. I trusted the people I worked with. It was, "Gosh, here I am at the eye of the storm." If I'd known what I know now, I'd have been worried.'

Despite such innocence, it did not take long, he says, for people to reach conclusions about the fire's underlying cause: 'The drive to produce plutonium, and cutting technical corners ... It happens in all industries: if you start getting too pushy, not taking care and pressing on, accidents happen.'

Morlais Harris left West Cumbria in 1960, taking a job at Manchester University's newly founded department of nuclear engineering. His father-in-law carried on working at Windscale until his retirement in 1972. The later criticisms of Windscale, and the civilian atomic energy project in general, from Friends of the Earth and Greenpeace caused Morlais Harris a great deal of irritation. He was particularly concerned by opportunities created by the developments in civil nuclear energy.

> I'd been brought up in the Welsh mining valleys which, like a lot of industrial areas, were blighted with pollution of the most appalling kind. The hillsides were covered in spoilheaps. The rivers ran black. It had been that way all my life. And I can never remember, at that time, anyone from the media class campaigning to clean up our environment. They didn't care. I just felt there was something skewed about it: here were these people going on about this industry who'd never raised so much as a squeak when large areas of the country were being ruined by the most dangerous, poisonous pollution. Where were they then?

Conclusion

Of the twenty or so Welsh scientists and engineers who were involved in the early years of the atomic energy programme, it is noteworthy that many came from working-class backgrounds. A number of them were the sons of miners, who had their aspirations raised either at school or at university. A large percentage of them went to a Welsh university. Many of them were from Swansea, and Swansea University looms large in the training of a number of the physicists and chemists who went on to work at Harwell and Aldermaston in the 1940s through to the 1960s.

Not surprisingly some of the scientists and engineers played a more important part in atomic energy programme than others. Some held senior positions while others had a more junior research role. Amongst the most prominent were the Harwell contingent of Lewis Roberts, Brian Flowers and Walter Marshall. They were brilliant scientists but also very able administrators. All three, as we have seen, also went on to hold high-level positions outside Harwell either as advisers to government on atomic energy matters, the senior civil service or higher education. At Aldermaston, the most influential of the Welsh scientists and engineers were Graham Hopkin, Ieuan Maddock, David Lewis and Percy White. All four, in different ways, contributed significantly to the pioneering initial work on the atomic bomb during the 1950s which led to the Hurricane test in October 1952. They also made important contributions to the later atomic and thermonuclear tests, as well as to the close technical relationship which developed with the United States from the late 1950s onwards following the signing of the MDA. Like their colleagues at Harwell, all four later held senior positions. Hopkin was to become the deputy director of Aldermaston. Ieuan Maddock became chief scientist to the Department of Trade and Industry. David Lewis became government chemist. And Percy White became a consultant to the Atomic Energy Authority and to the Department of Health. These positions were a testimony to the high regard of the scientists concerned and their reputation in the wider UK atomic energy field, as well as in the governments of the day. Many of the Welsh scientists, including Geoffrey Ellis, Aubrey Thomas, Gerald Davies and J. D. Davies, also continued to work at Aldermaston on the later modernisation of the Polaris programme.

THE BRITISH NUCLEAR PROGRAMME FROM CHEVALINE TO TRIDENT

In order to understand the role of Welsh scientists and engineers in the evolution of the British deterrent nuclear force after its early formative period it is important to understand the key features of the changes, including those in operational nuclear planning, that took place from the early 1960s through to the end of the Cold War in the 1990s. The focus of this chapter is on the Polaris Improvement Programme, leading to the development of Chevaline and subsequently the purchase of Trident missiles from the United States.[1]

The Moscow Criterion

Following the Nassau Agreement between Britain and the United States in 1963, the acquisition of Polaris raised important questions about UK strategic planning and how the nuclear force would be used. In order to be effective as a deterrent the chiefs of staff decided that it was imperative that the British nuclear force should be able to attack Moscow with an assurance of destruction.[2] The 'Moscow Criterion', as it became known, was based on a Joint Intelligence Committee (JIC) assessment from 1962. This assessment was based on what they believed the Soviet Union would consider 'unacceptable damage' and would:

> severely reduce the Soviet Union's economic and military strength
> in its struggle to overtake the United States and dominate the

world … [the JIC had] deliberately ignored the psychological, technical and political factors, but felt that it would not be unreasonable to say that the Soviet leaders would consider that the certain destruction of their five largest cities would put them at an unacceptable disadvantage in relation to the United States. The selection of the five largest cities was made on a points system, points being awarded for the following:

a. Size of population.
b. Civil and administrative centres.
c. Centres of economic control.
d. Military command posts.
e. Telecommunications centres.[3]

On this basis, Moscow was the most important one of the five and because of this the JIC assessment came to be known as the 'Moscow Criterion'. By the time Polaris began to be deployed in the North Atlantic in 1968 the target set had been revised again with an additional seven to eleven Soviet cities chosen for targeting. These again included Moscow and Leningrad (the two most populous cities of the USSR) with a minimum level of destruction of 50 per cent.[4] Of these cities the remainder had to have populations exceeding 300,000. These were the parameters for *independent* strategic nuclear targeting by the British Polaris force.[5]

One of the key UK nuclear planners, Sir Michael Quinlan, has argued that 'to allow the Soviet Union (a state system very much based upon central governmental authority) to enjoy perceived sanctuary for their capital and a considerable area around it would risk weakening whatever concern they might feel about the UK capability and resolve'.[6] With the Moscow Criterion at the centre of independent strategic targeting, military planners believed that it was essential to make sure the deterrent could get through the developing Soviet anti-ballistic missile (ABM) screen.[7]

As the Soviet Union began a concerted programme to protect its capital with anti-ballistic missiles in the late 1960s, the chiefs of staff argued that it remained necessary for the UK to continue to threaten

Moscow with an absolute 'assurance of destruction'.[8] There was scepticism that full-scale deployment of ABM systems around Soviet cities would occur given the high costs and limited effectiveness, but it was still seen as necessary to plan against the risk that the UK's deterrent would become ineffective against Soviet ABMs in the long term.[9] This sparked a lively debate amongst defence officials about the future of Polaris.

Should Polaris be replaced or improved?

One of the key questions for the Heath administration between 1970 and 1974 was whether to replace Polaris or to make improvements to overcome Soviet ABM defences. A meeting was planned for the end of July 1972 with Henry Kissinger, the US Secretary of State, in order to discover American feelings for a British request to purchase the US Poseidon submarine-launched ballistic missile (SLBM) system. Prior to this meeting Sir Burke Trend, the cabinet secretary, recommended that the Prime Minister, Chancellor of the Exchequer and Secretary of State for Defence should be fully briefed on the available courses open to the government at this juncture.[10] As part of the background to these major decisions a key briefing paper was given by the JIC.[11]

Although the results of this assessment remain classified, it seems detailed UK plans to target the Soviet Union were discussed. These plans were both in the context of joint targeting with the Americans ('deterrence in concert'), independent action ('independent deterrence') and possibly deterrence in conjunction with the French.[12] In light of the available evidence, it appears the chiefs of staff were able to maintain their preferred strategic targeting plan with the Moscow Criterion at its centre for the time being at least.[13]

However, in November 1975 (with Harold Wilson now back in power) both the JIC and the chiefs of staff (COS) were pointing out to ministers that they believed the current Polaris system was no longer fully effective at penetrating the improved Moscow ABM defences.[14] This had been considered a possibility since the early part of the 1960s but by 1975, with improvements to Soviet ABM systems, this was now considered by the JIC, COS and the nuclear weapons establishments on both sides of the Atlantic to be a strategic reality.[15] This realisation prompted a fundamental reassessment both of the current targeting requirements centred on the Moscow Criterion and of the British concept of independent nuclear deterrence. It was in this period that the JIC and COS as the 'primary keepers' of the prevailing strategic culture were to come under sustained political challenge.

Drawing on the findings of the substantial 1972 report by the JIC and the Polaris Policy Committee meeting late in 1975 (both of which examined alternate nuclear targeting priorities) the Chief of the Defence Staff (CDS), Sir Michael Carver, suggested targeting ten other cities west of the Ural Mountains, excluding Moscow entirely from the target list.[16] Carver believed that this 'would probably be regarded by the Russians as unacceptable damage'.[17] However the CDS also felt that if the Soviets believed Britain was attacking undefended targets then this would encourage them to extend the footprint of the current ABM defences.[18] In this event, Carver believed, removing the Moscow Criterion from the centre of British independent nuclear targeting should only be considered 'a temporary expedient'.[19]

By March 1976 Carver informed Roy Mason, the defence secretary, that the independent nuclear targeting plan, known as the National Retaliatory War Plan, should be altered to one of two options. This was either to fire from the Atlantic to attack ten cities other than Moscow, or to head into the Mediterranean to launch at Moscow.[20] These plans were contingent upon 'prevailing circumstances'. These were not explicitly stated by Carver but would likely to have included the number of Polaris submarines available and the political climate during times of tension.

The Chevaline programme: cabinet controversy

The arguments for re-targeting the UK strategic nuclear deterrent had a direct and sustained bearing on what became known as the 'Chevaline' programme to improve Polaris. This involved the development of a manoeuvrable warhead that would be able to defeat Soviet defences. With the cost of the Polaris improvement programme having risen from the 1972 estimates of £235m to an expected figure of £400m by

1975 it was under serious threat of cancellation.[21] With the government involved in yet another major defence review (initiated in 1974), Chevaline was not only under intense pressure to succeed but also to justify its continued rationale.

Both of these factors were under renewed scrutiny as the 1972 ABM Treaty and the 1974 protocol to the ABM Treaty (the 'Vladivostok Accords' – a result of the Superpower Strategic Arms Limitation Talks (SALT) negotiations) had limited Soviet ABMs to cover only the Soviet capital with a maximum 100 missile launchers. In order to justify the maintenance of the Moscow Criterion and with it the foundation for Chevaline the COS, backed by assessments of Soviet ABM capabilities from the JIC, began to mount a rearguard action to save Chevaline from cancellation. This serves to highlight intergovernmental disputes at the decision-making level and also how *military* decision-makers can decisively affect *political* policy choices.

The COS, the MoD and the JIC began this rearguard action by promoting the concept of the Moscow Criterion to the Prime Minister, Defence Secretary and Foreign Secretary. Pointedly the Chief of the Defence Staff wanted to exclude from the discussions on this issue the one remaining member of the executive ministerial committee on nuclear policy, Denis Healey, the Chancellor of the Exchequer (and former defence secretary).[22] Carver evidently felt that the alternative strategic plan of independent deterrence being suggested to Mason would leave Chevaline wide open to cancellation by the chancellor. However, John Mayne, Mason's private under-secretary, advised against this course of action. He counselled that to leave the chancellor out of the equation concerning the re-targeting of Polaris would be, 'madness … inspite [*sic*] of the dangers'.[23]

Mayne suggested Mason simply restate to Healey the argument given back in September 1974 for retaining Chevaline, namely that cancellation would dilute both the deterrent effect on the Soviet Union whilst concomitantly damaging relations with the United States who 'in past discussions stressed their wish to see Britain have a powerful deterrent capability'.[24] There does not seem to have been any further overt political discussion by Mason regarding targeting policy. Instead he chose to accept the advice of his chiefs of staff in regard to the Moscow Criterion.

In line with the sentiments of the chiefs, on 18 November 1975, Mayne produced for Mason a memorandum suggesting that until Chevaline was introduced into service Polaris would be ineffective from the end of the year.[25] These discussions between senior members of the civil service and government regarding re-targeting continued to gather political momentum. At a meeting between Sir John Hunt (the cabinet secretary), Secretary of State for Defence Mason, and CDS, Sir Michael Carver, a little over a week later on 27 November, it was agreed that the chancellor should not be told about the minute circulated from the COS to the prime minister revising the COS criteria for strategic nuclear deterrence.[26] All three hoped that Healey could be kept away from the conclusions by the COS that deterrence could also be demonstrated if Polaris were re-targeted to ten cities *excluding* Moscow.

This was further discussed prior to a meeting of the Public Expenditure Survey Committee (PESC) due to take place on 5 December. There it was decided that if the prime minister wished to see the chancellor informed of these conclusions then a disclaimer would be issued by them that Healey did not 'need to know' about the re-targeting options. At a subsequent high level MoD meeting on 1 June 1976 it was further suggested that rather than targeting ten cities west of the Ural Mountains, five could be targeted and this could also fulfil the criteria of deterrence. Mason again made the case for continuing to develop Chevaline, maintaining that it was essential to be able to continue to attack Moscow in the long term. However, emphasising the competitive nature of defence procurement policy – even in the highly prized nuclear field, in the climate of financial austerity brought about by the defence review he felt that it would be necessary to remind the prime minister of this need.[27]

At this meeting Sir Edward Ashmore, the chief of the naval staff, reminded the group that what 'constituted a credible deterrent was political'.[28] Still it is unclear why five cities and not ten were now being considered an effective political deterrent. It is likely that targeting five cities and excluding Moscow from the target list would have led to further doubts placed against the case for retaining Chevaline. The Treasury had been absent from the meeting and would very likely have seized on this relaxation of the criteria for national deterrence to press the MoD to cancel the improvement programme and derail the 'critical momentum' that was building behind the retention of the Moscow Criterion and the need for Chevaline. Moreover this would have reframed one of the key parameters of British nuclear policy.

At least equal consideration would have been given to the reduced number of Soviet cities to be targeted by Polaris. With twenty cities having been considered to be a 'minimum deterrent' in 1964 why twelve years later was ten and then five considered to be acceptable?[29] Perhaps more than anything this clearly indicates that the UK politico-military concept of 'minimum deterrence' was a moveable feast which rested in large measure on force levels and military capabilities rather than a hard rule based on certainty.

Mason also expressed concerns that this review of the criteria for deterrence would be leaked.[30] A government leak threatened to bring out into the open the question of what constituted a politically acceptable minimum deterrent. This would cause further embarrassment to an administration battling industrial unrest and inflation in the domestic economy. Two weeks later Mason informed the new prime minister, James Callaghan, of these re-targeting recommendations with a view to informing the foreign secretary, Anthony Crosland, and Chancellor Healey.[31] Although it is not known for sure if this revision by the COS was accepted by the government, David Owen (Crosland's successor as foreign secretary in 1977) suggests that there would have been no political reason not to accept this advice. He himself had no knowledge of these discussions when he became foreign secretary.[32]

To question the basis of a minimum national deterrent coupled with the risk of government leaks could have proved extremely damaging to the confidence of those involved with the Chevaline programme and would also have dented nuclear relations with the United States. It would also have given critics of the British nuclear programme, including those in the Labour Party with links to the Campaign for Nuclear Disarmament (CND), added ammunition to attack the foundations of the nuclear deterrent.

Still it was argued during this meeting that if Chevaline was cancelled then the resources that were being provided would be freed up and could be reallocated to a successor system.[33] Under these terms of reference Mason suggested that any talk of successor systems 'should cease forthwith, at least for two years. Such talk would undermine Chevaline; and the possibility was politically out of the question.'[34] To assist with the rearguard action to preserve Chevaline, in June 1976 Mason agreed to approach Tony Crosland, whose term as foreign secretary lasted just ten months, armed with a full presentation team prior to recommending to the prime minister that Chevaline should be allowed to continue at 'full speed'.[35] This was duly granted.

With regard to these deliberations, as Lord Healey commented in a 2011 BBC documentary,

> They didn't want to tell me because they knew I understood the issue perfectly well and would cancel … and that's one of the worries I think ministers must have about civil servants, that they will withhold information which they think will lead to a decision they don't like.[36]

He also stated that it was 'disgraceful' that this was done, even on grounds of national security. When asked how he felt about the implication that even he, as Chancellor of the Exchequer and a former defence secretary, could not be trusted, he replied: 'Not be trusted to agree with them. Well, sod them!' Healey went further claiming: 'If civil servants conceal the most important facts about the decisions you have to take, they're betraying their country. It's a form of treason.'[37]

Whilst not going as far as treason, Lord Owen too was critical of the civil service role in these deliberations, claiming

> it's quite a disgraceful judgement because he [Healey] did have a need to know. I think Sir John Hunt [the former cabinet secretary] crossed the line and he should not have been party to the decision to freeze Denis Healey out … That was, I think, a reprehensible decision, and it should be made clear to future cabinet secretaries where the line is. And he crossed the line.[38]

The stakes were high. When asked if this could have brought down Harold Wilson's government Healey answered 'Conceivably, I think so, yes.'[39] Chevaline was revealed publicly in 1980, and deployed from 1982 until 1996.

The role of key officials and the Trident debate

At the beginning of 1978, by which time Harold Wilson had been replaced as prime minister by James Callaghan, consideration was being given in the Ministry of Defence to a number of options for a successor system. These included cruise missiles, Trident or an indigenous SLBM programme capable of carrying multiple re-entry vehicles (MIRVs).[40] In light of this two working parties were formed to advise this four-man committee. One working party was set up under Professor Sir Ronald Mason, chief scientific advisor to the MoD. Its remit was to examine the technical options regarding Polaris replacements. The second was chaired by Sir Anthony Duff, deputy under-secretary at the Foreign and Commonwealth Office (FCO). This party was charged with a far-reaching study of the wider international implications of each replacement system.[41]

The work of these two groups was to be left alone and free from ministerial input at any stage. This even included the MoD who had been pleased to have authority over the 'nuts and bolts' aspect of both studies. However, the two groups were to be monitored from Whitehall by a select band of senior civil servants representing the FCO, MoD and Treasury along with Sir Clive Rose of the cabinet secretariat.[42] There was also a significant military overview in the shape of chief of the defence staff, Marshal of the Royal Air Force, Sir Neil Cameron.[43]

Given the problems encountered with Chevaline, as we have seen, the Moscow Criterion was not assumed to have overriding merit and, instead, alternative counter-city strategic planning was openly discussed, including targeting the next nine largest cities in the Soviet Union.[44] The Duff-Mason Report was submitted in December 1978 and recommended that the deterrent be retained if it could be afforded.[45] It offered a revealing insight into British strategic culture when arguing:

The essential point to be made about the effect on our status is that this cannot be judged in the abstract. While it might be argued that if we were now contemplating becoming a nuclear power this would add little to our status, it cannot be assumed that abandonment of our capability would have a similarly limited effect. We were the first state to perceive the implications of atomic power, and the third state to become an effective nuclear power. If we were to turn our back on this history and abandon our role as an NWS, this would be regarded internationally as a momentous step in British history. Our possession of nuclear weapons gives us a standing in world affairs which we would not otherwise have ... Finally, our status as a nuclear power is important for our relationship to other medium powers, since we have lagged behind them in other indicators of prestige ... especially ... in relation to West Germany ... and to France. As to the general correlation between international status and a nuclear capability, the examples of Japan and West Germany suggest that economic indicators are nowadays more important for influence than strategic ones, and that our efforts and resources might better be concentrated on the former.[46]

The Duff-Mason Report also unequivocally stated that: 'Our existing strategic nuclear force has the unique purpose of deterring the Soviet Union ... there will be insufficient interaction between British and Chinese interests.' This was despite a comment in the margin of the report questioning whether the handover of Hong Kong to the Chinese would go peaceably. Other credible scenarios were also seen as possible.

But we have long since given up the role of World Policeman to the United States, and while we would be expected to give political backing to the United States in such a crisis, a British nuclear contribution would not be required ... it is possible to postulate scenarios of major political change within European states ... and, at the other extreme, of a dramatic movement towards European integration, which could prove incompatible with a defence arrangement on existing lines.[47]

Part II of the Duff-Mason Report outlined four 'interrelated purposes' for a British nuclear deterrent. These were:

a. a numerical contribution to the assigned forces of NATO;
b. the contribution of a second centre of nuclear decision-making to Alliance deterrence of the Soviet Union;
c. a capability for the independent defence of national interests;
d. political status and influence.[48]

In terms of independence it was stated that:

> We must retain sole national control over the order to fire our nuclear weapons ... This view carries implications for possible cooperation with another state or states in the procurement and maintenance of a strategic capability. We must be able to sustain our capability nationally for a period of time [at least one year], to guard against the risk that a partner might seek to neutralise our capability for independent action by cutting off his support during a crisis.[49]

This again harks back to 1940 and the Battle of Britain when Britain faced the might of Nazi Germany alone. The primary keepers of British strategic culture had to guard against a repeat combined with the potential for nuclear blackmail and a possible choice whether to surrender or die reflecting the continuing dominance of a pervading 'realist' mind-set.

Duff-Mason also echoed a number of relevant points regarding the uniqueness of British diplomatic and strategic culture, including what might be lost if Britain were to give up its status as a nuclear power. They argued that this would dent Britain's standing in Europe and the world in several ways with a clear conviction that France should not be left as Western Europe's sole nuclear weapons state – with the fate of Europe potentially out of British hands.[50] Despite the relative smallness of the British arsenal compared to the superpowers there were likely similarities between them in politico-military outlook when faced with rational judgements of defeat or surrender and:

It cannot be assumed that (given our much greater vulnerability than the United States to nuclear attack) that a British
Government would be readier than the United States President to
engage in nuclear escalation that might provoke Soviet retaliation
against our territory, even in circumstances in which British forces
(like United States forces) might be facing defeat in combat.[51]

The 'second centre' of alliance nuclear decision-making, as outlined,
was balanced against a situation where there could conceivably be a
long-term decline in the US commitment to Europe. Were this to occur
then British and French nuclear forces, with their differing strategic
cultures, might well come into play to a far greater extent in a situation
not unlike 1940. In words that echoed the memory of both world wars
the Duff-Mason report stated:

> Ultimate deterrence is perceived to work, because no nuclear weap-
> ons state (NWS) can feel confident enough to act on a judgement
> that an adversary, seeing the painful destruction of all that he most
> valued, would withhold retaliation on account of some cool calcu-
> lation based on ethics and utility.[52]

Duff-Mason also argued that the Soviet Union placed great value on
some cities, particularly Leningrad and Moscow which they judged was
based on 'both Russian tradition and preservationist practice'.[53]

A digest of the main points of the report was produced for the
COS with a 'military emphasis' as a background for discussions by the
Defence Policy Staff (DPS) in August 1979.[54] This report acted as a
comprehensive reassessment of British independent nuclear deterrence
again centred upon the Moscow Criterion. The Duff-Mason Report was
broken down into three categories and the DPS expressed reservations
over a number of its conclusions. The categories were:

1. The politico-military requirement;
2. Criteria for deterrence;
3. System options and their implications.

The politico-military requirement discussed the 'general concept of deterrence, the strategy of flexible response imposed on the Alliance by the establishment of strategic parity between the superpowers, and Soviet strategic philosophy with its emphasis on pre-emption, survival and war-winning'.[55]

The discussion then focused on the theory of deterrence by medium nuclear powers such as Britain and France; with emphasis on Britain's contribution to NATO. This contribution was defined partly as numerical, in providing a second-centre of decision-making, a capability to act independently and lastly the political status and influence provided by such capabilities. It was the second and third categories that drove the force levels and capabilities, such as those for Chevaline, and the Moscow Criterion.[56]

Furthermore, in one of the most extensive expositions of the British concept of independent nuclear deterrence so far released, the DPS stated that: 'credibility resides partly in the material and organisational ability to mount an unacceptably damaging strike whatever the conditions, and partly in the will to do so'.[57] The DPS continued:

> These two factors support each other; and the combination of them must sufficiently impress the Soviet Union to ensure deterrence. We would add only that Soviet leaders now, and probably in the future, are realists ... they will not be impressed – or deterred – by strategic systems that have a very low chance of inflicting unacceptable damage against the defensive measures of the day.[58]

The DPS instead produced their own assessment of the damage deemed necessary to deter the Soviet Union. They argued that: 'There will be many circumstances, particularly in situations of advanced escalation, where UK strategic forces capable only of Option 3b ('30 bangs in 30 places') would be insufficient to deter a Soviet strike aimed at, say, knocking the UK out of a war.'[59]

The DPS placed this view in an historical setting. With over 20 million casualties resulting from the Nazi invasion of the Soviet Union during the Second World War, and a similar number killed during the Stalinist purges between 1930 and 1950, 'this must give at least a measure of the threshold with which UK planning has to deal'.[60] In this context, the assessment of the criteria for deterrence articulated by the DPS had to be significantly larger than thirty cities, 'if a crude criteria of megadeaths is to apply'.[61] Instead the DPS pressed for the retention of the Moscow Criterion as the capital retained the greatest importance in terms of population as well as industry and centralised command and control. It was felt the loss of the Moscow area would be a blow from which the Soviet Union would not recover. This would then place them in a position of long-term inferiority between both the US and China.[62]

Mason's part of the report was savaged by Denis Healey in a revealing commentary on bureaucratic politics within the British civil service:

> David Owen and I both felt that the Chevaline programme was too expensive. We didn't need to be able to hit Moscow. But again, I think, the thing slipped through, after this very perfunctory and almost meaningless paper by the Chief Scientist. This is not, after all, to do with technology; this is to do with how likely you think a certain contingency, how you think the other side will react to their knowledge that you have certain capabilities. That's what it's all about. It's nothing whatever to do with scientists or, with respect, with generals.[63]

Callaghan, however, was of the opinion that a replacement system was needed and was prepared to make a case to the British public. In making this case he expected opposition from within his own party. It was decided that an informal request should be made to the United States for the Trident C-4 but without further commitment. With the results of the Duff-Mason Report fresh in his mind, and with the endorsement of his nuclear committee colleagues, Callaghan approached US President Carter between 4 and 6 January 1979 during the four power summit at Guadeloupe. Carter reacted favourably to this request, although Callaghan made it clear that no formal decision had yet been made.[64] However, Callaghan lost the May 1979 general election and it was left to Margaret Thatcher's Conservative government to plot a way forward.

The Trident decision

Using the Duff-Mason Report as a basis for a decision regarding a successor system, Margaret Thatcher formed her own cabinet sub-committee – MISC 7 – in order to debate the points more fully and to formulate a strategy. To aid MISC 7 the CDS, Sir Terence Lewin, and the group of senior civil servants who had supervised the Duff-Mason investigations were reconstituted. On 6 December 1979, a formal decision was made by the MISC 7 committee for the government to try to procure the Trident C-4 system, minus the warheads and submarines, both of which would be built in Britain. This decision was later brought to the attention of the full cabinet and on 15 July 1980 the cabinet was informed that the sale of Trident had been agreed by the US.[65]

Prior to the formal signing, President Carter stated that the US desire to see the bi-partisan nuclear relationship extended as the 'United States attaches significant importance to the nuclear deterrent capability of the United Kingdom and to close cooperation between our two Governments in maintaining and modernising that capability'.[66] This point was echoed by Harold Brown (the US defence secretary) to his opposite number, Francis Pym. Brown noted that the Trident purchase represented 'an important contribution to our continued close defense co-operation, which enhances the security not only of the United States and the United Kingdom, but of our allies and the world generally'.[67]

The deal also held open the possibility of the British purchase of the Trident D-5 version, which had a longer range and greater payload capacity, although this was still in development in the United States.[68] When Ronald Reagan became US president in January 1981 he made it clear that his new Republican administration would seek to modernise US strategic nuclear forces. On 24 August 1981 Casper Weinberger, the new defence secretary, informed Margaret Thatcher that America was going to speed up the development of the Trident II (D-5) programme. This meant 'bringing it into the British time frame' and they soon declared that they would make this available.[69] On 1 October President Reagan made a formal offer of the Trident D-5 to the British government.[70]

In November 1981 an inner cabinet committee met to discuss what to do. Margaret Thatcher records: 'We argued out all the questions between us; and all the arguments which would be raised in the outside world were discussed, including some feeble and unrealistic ones.'[71] These 'feeble' and 'unrealistic' arguments were the impact on public opinion in choosing a more powerful missile, whether the upgraded D-5 could be kept out of future arms control negotiations (as had been possible hitherto), or whether the government could purchase fewer missiles. One unnamed minister also raised the possibility of 'whether the UK could afford to maintain an independent strategic nuclear deterrent at all' but was quickly overruled by the prime minister.[72] Both President Reagan and Defense Secretary Weinberger were keen for Britain to accept D-5.[73] The formal agreement was signed on 19 October 1982.[74]

The decision to procure the D-5 was announced to parliament by John Nott in the following terms:

> After detailed consideration here, and with the United States, we have now decided also to purchase the Trident II D5, instead of the Trident I C4 missile system, from the United States. The number of warheads that the Trident II D5 missile will carry, and therefore Trident's striking power, remains wholly a matter of choice for the British Government. Our intention is that the move to D5 will not involve any significant change in the planned total number of warheads than we originally envisaged for our Trident I C4 force. The reasons for our choice of Trident II are briefly as follows. Just as the Polaris system will, by the mid-1990s, have been in service for approaching 30 years and will have reached the end of its operational life, so the Trident system must remain operational until 2020 – that is, 40 years from now.[75]

The Trident purchase held out the possibility of contributing to a more flexible counterforce nuclear posture. Writing shortly before his death, Michael Quinlan, a key figure in the development of British nuclear policy, argued that the reference to 'Soviet state power' mentioned in a Defence Open Government Document in 1980 was:

deliberately chosen – partly with ethical concerns in mind – to convey that, while, cities could not be guaranteed immunity, the UK approach to deterrent threat and operational planning in the Trident era would not rest on crude counter city or counter-population concepts.[76]

This was an important change, which went largely unrecognised by the public at the time. Quinlan also argued that:

Purely in weight of strike potential the United Kingdom could have been content with less than Trident could offer, even in the eight-RV C.4 version originally chosen (let alone the twelve-RV D.5 version to which the United Kingdom switched in early 1982, when it had become clear that the United States was committed to proceed with its acquisition and deployment). Both the original choice and the switch were driven in large measure by the long-term financial and logistic benefits of commonality with the United States.[77]

In an interview held prior to the 1987 general election Margaret Thatcher publicly restated her views on nuclear deterrence and a clear exposition of British strategic culture, which again harked back to memories of the Battle of Britain. She also highlighted the fact that the opposition Labour Party led by the Welsh MP Neil Kinnock had adopted a policy of unilateral nuclear disarmament.[78] Thatcher stated her belief that if Labour won the election:

the damage done to NATO, the damage done to liberty because Britain has always stood for liberty, the damage done to Britain's defences, would be so deep, so fundamental that they [the chiefs of staff] could no longer be responsible for carrying the burden of defence ... that is a fundamental part of the way of life in which I believe ... Britain isn't just another country. We wouldn't have grown to an empire if we were just another European country of the size and strength that we were. It was Britain that stood when everyone else surrendered and if Britain pulls out of that commitment, it is as if one of the pillars of the temple had collapsed. Because we are one of the pillars of freedom. And hitherto everyone, including past Labour Prime Ministers, have known that Britain would stand and Britain had a nuclear weapon.[79]

Domestic opposition to nuclear weapons

While there was strong establishment support for British nuclear weapons, the 1980s saw a new wave of anti-nuclear sentiment emerge. The NATO decision in 1979 to deploy Cruise and Pershing missiles in a number of European countries (including Britain), in response to the Soviet deployment of its SS-20 missile, caused great anxiety in certain sections of British society. The Campaign for Nuclear Disarmament (CND) in the late 1950s and early 1960s had organised a major social movement against nuclear weapons and had been successful in changing Labour Party policy for a time in favour of unilateral disarmament. The movement declined somewhat after a number of nuclear arms control agreements in the 1960s and 1970s shifted the emphasis towards multilateral, rather than unilateral, disarmament. The arrival of Cruise missiles in Britain in the early 1980s, however, led to a renewal of anxiety about the possibilities of nuclear war.

This was reflected particularly in a campaign that began in Wales against the deployment of US Cruise missiles at Greenham Common. Four women from west Wales organised a march of forty or so, mainly women, from Cardiff to Greenham Common in late August 1981.[80] The four women were Ann Pettit, Helen John, Sue Lent and Karmen Thomas. The original idea for the walk came from Ann Pettit, a French teacher, from Llanpumsaint. She was inspired by a similar women's walk from Copenhagen to Paris. She was a young mother concerned about nuclear waste and the dangers of nuclear war at the time. Helen John was a midwife with five children who shared Ann Pettit's concerns. Sue Lent was twenty-nine at the time and a graduate of Cardiff University. She took her baby with her on the walk. The fourth original organiser of the walk was Karmen Thomas, a close friend of Ann Pettit from

Ammanford.[81] Karmen was put in charge of the liaison with the police during the march and she also accompanied Ann on a visit to Moscow in 1983 to visit peace movements in the Soviet Union.

The route of the march took them from Cardiff, passing the Royal Ordnance factory at Llanishen, where components of nuclear weapons were manufactured. They then walked through Newport to Chepstow, passing an American arms depot at Caerwent, where stocks of chemical weapons were kept. From there they continued through Bristol, Bath, Melksham, Devizes, Marlborough, Hungerford and on to Newbury. On the way they made a detour to the US base at Welford where tactical nuclear weapons were based. The 120-mile walk took ten days to complete and when they arrived on 5 September they delivered a letter of protest to the base commandant. The letter stated: 'We have undertaken this action because we believe that the nuclear arms race constitutes the greatest threat ever faced by the human race and our living planet.' 'The Women for Life on Earth', as they called themselves, then set up a camp outside the base and were soon joined by women from all parts of the UK and abroad, including famous women such as Julie Christie, Yoko Ono, Susannah York and Sheila Hancock. As the campaign grew protesters adopted a range of non-violent activities designed to disrupt the work at the base and to highlight their opposition to the deployment of the missiles in Britain and nuclear weapons in general. At its height in April 1983 over 70,000 joined hands around the 14-mile perimeter fence in what has been described as 'the largest women's demonstration in modern history'.[82] Sadly, one young woman from Newcastle Emlyn, Helen Thomas, was killed in a road accident outside the base in August 1989.

Although the women's peace camp remained until 2000, the conclusion of the Intermediate Range Nuclear Forces (INF) Agreement in 1987 between the United States and the Soviet Union, led to a lessening of public anxiety. As missiles on both sides were withdrawn, some protesters stayed on to try to ensure that the common land at Greenham was handed back to the people of Newbury. The INF Agreement itself became an important milestone on the road that led to the end of the Cold War in the late 1980s.

TABLE 2 Joint Anglo-American nuclear tests 1962–91*

Test series	Test name	Date (GCT)	Location	Test type	Yield (kt)	Purpose
Nougat	Pampas	1-Mar-62	NTS	Shaft	9.5 kt	Accidental release of radioactivity detected off-site
Roller Coaster	Double Tracks	15-May-62	NAFR	Surface	0	Storage-transportation safety experiment, measured plutonium dispersal risk
Roller Coaster	Clean Slate I	25-May-62	NAFR	Surface	0	Storage-transportation safety experiment, measured plutonium dispersal risk
Roller Coaster	Clean Slate II	31-May-62	NAFR	Surface	0	Storage-transportation safety experiment, measured plutonium dispersal risk
Roller Coaster	Clean Slate III	9-Jun-62	NAFR	Surface	0	Storage-transportation safety experiment, measured plutonium dispersal risk
Storax	Tendrac	7-Dec-62	NTS	Shaft	<20 kt	
Whetstone	Cormorant	17-Jul-64	NTS	Shaft	<20 kt	Accidental release of radioactivity detected on-site only
Whetstone	Courser	25-Sep-64	NTS	Shaft	0	
Flintlock	Charcoal	10-Sep-65	NTS	Shaft	20–200 kt	
Arbor	Fallon	23-May-74	NTS	Shaft	20–200 kt	First test of the Chevaline warhead (TK-100?)
Anvil	Banon	26-Aug-76	NTS	Shaft	20–150 kt	Chevaline?
Cresset	Fondutta	11-Apr-78	NTS	Shaft	20–150 kt	Chevaline?
Quicksilver	Quargel	18-Nov-78	NTS	Shaft	20–150 kt	Chevaline?

(continued)

Test series	Test name	Date (GCT)	Location	Test type	Yield (kt)	Purpose
Quicksilver	Nessel	29-Aug-79	NTS	Shaft	20–150 kt	Chevaline?
Tinderbox	Colwick	26-Apr-80	NTS	Shaft	20–150 kt	Chevaline?
Guardian	Dutchess	24-Oct-80	NTS	Shaft	<20 kt	
Guardian	Serpa	17-Dec-80	NTS	Shaft	20–150 kt	Chevaline?
Praetorian	Rousanne	12-Nov-81	NTS	Shaft	20–150 kt	Chevaline?
Praetorian	Gibne	25-Apr-82	NTS	Shaft	20–150 kt	Chevaline?
Phalanx	Armada	22-Apr-83	NTS	Shaft	<20 kt	Trident primary test?
Fusileer	Mundo	1-May-84	NTS	Shaft	20–150 kt	Trident?
Grenadier	Egmont	9-Dec-84	NTS	Shaft	20–150 kt	Trident?
Charioteer	Kinibito	5-Dec-85	NTS	Shaft	20–150 kt	Trident?
Charioteer	Darwin	25-Jun-86	NTS	Shaft	20–150 kt	Trident?
Musketeer	Midland	16-Jul-87	NTS	Shaft	20–150 kt	Trident?
Aqueduct	Barnwell	18-Dec-89	NTS	Shaft	20–150 kt	Likely Trident full yield test, seismic magnitude Mb 5.7
Sculpin	Houston	14-Nov-90	NTS	Shaft	20–150 kt	Likely Trident full yield test, seismic magnitude Mb 5.7
Julin	Bristol	26-Nov-91	NTS	Shaft	<20 kt	Trident low yield option test?

* Source: The Nuclear Weapon Archive: A Guide to Nuclear Weapons (*https://nuclearweaponarchive.org*). NAFR refers to Nellis Airforce Range (Nevada), and NTS refers to the Nevada Test Site.

The post-Cold War period

With the end of the Cold War and the collapse of the Soviet Union the rationale for Britain's nuclear deterrent posture was challenged. This led to a number of changes to nuclear policy in the years ahead. In 1998 as part of the Strategic Defence Review (SDR) conducted by the Labour government it was decided to operate only forty-eight warheads (all in the kiloton range) in each submarine rather than the ninety-six the Conservative government had planned and to put the Trident nuclear force on 'several days readiness' to fire. Coupled with this it was also decided to de-target the Trident force (although plans remained for their employment) and to withdraw the air-launched WE-177 gravity bomb. It has also been suggested that rather than take its full complement of sixteen missiles on normal deterrent patrols now only twelve are loaded, armed with five or less warheads apiece.[83]

The 1998 SDR stated that:

> Britain's Trident force provides an operationally independent strategic and sub-strategic nuclear capability in support of NATO's strategy of war prevention and as the ultimate guarantee of our national security. In current circumstances, nuclear forces continue to make a unique contribution to ensuring stability and preventing crisis escalation. They also help guard against any possible re-emergence of a strategic scale threat to our security.[84]

Additionally the UK/US Trident force remains, the review states, the only one committed to NATO, and Britain's is the only European nuclear force assigned to the alliance due to the fact that France continued to operate its nuclear forces on a national basis only (although under President Sarkozy it had agreed to rejoin NATO's integrated military structure which it left in 1966).

The decisions taken in the 1998 SDR were subsequently amended somewhat with the efforts of NATO, publicly evidenced in the alliance's mutating strategic concepts, simultaneously geared less towards military solutions in a dynamic security environment. As George Robertson stated shortly before his departure as NATO secretary general in 2004, 'military means are only one instrument in the armoury. Maybe even the least important of those elements that are needed … Diplomatic pressure, economic pressure, communications pressure is going to have to be deployed.'[85] 'Soft' security issues are thus having to be accorded increasing priority over traditional 'hard' strategic concerns at which level nuclear deterrence primarily (if not solely) functions.

The White Paper issued by the government in December 2006 to explain the Trident renewal decision further announced that the explosive yield of the warheads was being reduced to 'considerably below that of the standard warhead'.[86] It also made clear, in what it described as 'Five enduring principles', the underpinnings of the Trident replacement decision:

1. To deter nuclear attack and prevent nuclear blackmail and acts of aggression that cannot be accomplished by other means;
2. A 'minimum' deterrent in line with the 1998 SDR and changes in the global security environment leading to the reduction of the number of operationally available warheads from 200 to fewer than 160;
3. A continuing policy of strategic ambiguity regarding potential employment including the potential for first use;
4. The assignment of Trident to NATO in support of collective security for the Euro-Atlantic area. This in turn forms part of the alliance's overall strategy and the nuclear guarantee afforded by the British commitment;
5. A 'second centre' of nuclear decision within the NATO alliance. Potential adversaries might be prepared to 'gamble' that neither the US or France would retaliate to an attack on the UK or upon its allies. Britain could therefore act alone 'where supreme national interests are at stake'.[87]

Whilst many of the arguments for the retention of a British nuclear capability still resonate from the days of the Cold War there were additional material changes to strategic doctrine, including the revocation of a 'sub-strategic' capability for Trident. In a speech at Kings College in January 2007, the Secretary of State for Defence, Des Browne, stated:

> [Nuclear weapons] should not be used for anything other than deterring extreme threats to our national security. The U.K. has in fact never sought to use our nuclear weapons as a means of provoking or coercing others. We will never do so. Nor are our weapons intended or designed for military use during conflict. Indeed, we have deliberately chosen to stop using the term 'sub-strategic Trident', applied previously to a possible limited use of our weapons. I would like to take this opportunity to reaffirm that the U.K. would only consider using nuclear weapons in the most extreme situations of self-defence.[88]

Remarks made by Lord Drayson, parliamentary under-secretary for state in the Ministry of Defence, during debates in the House of Lords firm up this reasoning. Drayson commented that 'any conceivable use of our nuclear weapons – at whatever scale – would necessarily be strategic, both in intent and effect. Indeed we have deliberatively discontinued the use of the term sub-strategic, in the sense that it had been used previously to apply to a possible, limited use of our nuclear weapons.'[89]

Despite these modifications of policy, however, both Conservative-led and Labour governments and their officials have continued to believe that a British nuclear force was needed as a hedge against the uncertainty which lay ahead. The 2007 Defence White Paper reflected the government's belief that 'in a global environment still with so much uncertainty and potential danger now was not the time to decide to abandon entirely a capability which the United Kingdom had possessed for half a century'.[90]

Through the course of the debate on Trident renewal/replacement two rationales which have long been government policy were placed under renewed scrutiny. The first, described above, concerned itself with the *national* purpose of the force as a 'minimum independent deterrent'.

The second relates to the political guarantee afforded to NATO under Article 5 of the North Atlantic Treaty of 1949 whereby an attack against one member is considered an attack against all.

Despite its commitment to NATO, Britain retains its right of withdrawal for its nuclear forces for use on a national basis. Under what circumstances such a withdrawal would occur is not clear and any explicit statement on this has been avoided ever since the Nassau Agreement was signed in 1962. The reasons for the retention of this clause are threefold. First, it allows the British government to be able to make its own judgements regarding the security of the state under conditions of last resort (i.e. nuclear attack by a foreign actor) without formal deference to the views of a foreign government (including the United States).[91] Secondly, it has allowed Britain to develop its own strategic doctrine and bolster its role as a 'second centre' of nuclear decision-making in the NATO alliance. Thirdly, it makes it implicit that the use of British nuclear weapons by NATO would ultimately be a decision taken at national level and not forced on the government by NATO's Nuclear Planning Group (NPG) or executive Military Committee (MC).[92] To facilitate this arrangement the command and control chain (C^2) remains under national control.[93]

Due to the intimacy of the long-standing 'special nuclear relationship', which forms a key part of the wider special relationship between Britain and America, the US and UK may also operate a separate targeting set to that of NATO. These might include targets deemed of greater priority to them as individual states or due to involvement in situations where NATO is not involved or even where authorisation for nuclear use has been blocked by the NPG or MC. Alongside these multilateral plans there is also likely to be a plan for UK national action in circumstances where neither NATO nor the United States is involved. This is perhaps the least likely of all three strategic nuclear targeting contingency plans but is nevertheless provided for under the 'supreme national interests' clause of the 1962 Nassau Agreement. This last plan however remains something of a remnant to the days when Britain had global interests to protect, some of which did not coincide with American national interests. It is worth noting that the last time Britain engaged in a major action where America was not directly involved, the Falklands conflict of 1982, the UK could still call upon US assets and full diplomatic support.

Significantly, in 2009 the Foreign Office published a report entitled 'Lifting the Nuclear Shadow: Creating the Conditions for Abolishing Nuclear Weapons' in which it was indicated that there were some 'powerful arguments for reducing the role of nuclear weapons solely to deterring the use of nuclear weapons by others' and that, in general, it was important to reduce the saliency of nuclear weapons in national security policies.[94] The argument for retaining its nuclear capability was now made in very broad terms:

> It related in essence to the unsettled and still-anarchic character of the international environment; to the continued intention of the United Kingdom to be a major load-bearing actor in it, and to have the confidence to accept responsibilities and risks accordingly; to the impossibility of predicting dangers far enough ahead for it to be acceptable to defer provision against them until they had become evident; and to the effective finality of any decision to withdraw from the possession of a nuclear armoury.[95]

As such there was a strong conviction amongst officials that it would be necessary to extend the service life of the Trident system to around 2042, continuing its close collaboration with the United States – a policy that continued with the publication of the 'Strategic Defence and Security Review' in 2010.[96] In 1996 Britain had signed the Comprehensive Test Ban Treaty which banned all nuclear explosions for both civilian and military purposes in all environments. Given the determination to retain a British nuclear capability, however, a way had to be found to keep the components of the force up to date and safe over time. To achieve this, the government purchased the Bull Sequana X1000 supercomputer from Atos to simulate nuclear explosions. The computer allowed scientists to use digital modelling to redesign and change components of the nuclear force when it became necessary in order to maintain the viability of the deterrent force.[97]

In 2016, with growing difficulties with Putin's Russia and inter-national uncertainty, there was a report by the Nuclear Information Service that AWE Aldermaston was engaged in a programme to replace the W76 Trident warhead with a new more accurate and powerful warhead designed to allow Britain to choose a wider range of targets by giving greater control over the height of detonation.[98] It was also reported that a joint working group had been set up with American and British experts to allow collaboration on the programme and that the new warhead had undergone tests at the Sandia National Laboratories in the United States. Press reports indicated that AWE's design studies for the new warhead had already cost £85 million by this stage.[99] Following on from this in July 2017 the House of Commons supported the May government's policy of purchasing a fleet of four Dreadnought submarines, renewing the UK's nuclear deterrent force for the next thirty years.

Conclusion

Although states acquire nuclear weapons for different reasons, the study of the British nuclear experience from the Second World War suggests that the beliefs of influential political, military and scientific figures are of crucial importance. In the case of Britain, fears of an existential threat from Germany in the Second World War and Cold War concerns about the vulnerability of the UK in an anarchic nuclear world led to a strong and consistent view amongst the elite that nuclear weapons had distinct utility. In particular, governments of both left and right shared the belief held by the chiefs of staff that Britain had an 'inalienable right' to such weapons. There was also a strong conviction that, although Britain's power was declining, nuclear weapons could provide status and prestige that its continuing perceived role (and self-identity) as a great power required. Contemporary geopolitical changes and renewed East–West tensions have helped to maintain the traditional British belief in the utility of nuclear weapons. In the story of maintaining the viability of the British nuclear deterrent Welsh scientists and engineers continued to play an important role.

THE INVOLVEMENT OF WELSH SCIENTISTS AND ENGINEERS IN THE BRITISH NUCLEAR PROGRAMME FROM THE 1960s TO THE PRESENT DAY

Welsh chemists and the development of 'new materials'

As we have seen in the previous chapter, an important part of the Chevaline and Trident programmes from the 1960s to the 1990s was the 'hardening' of the warheads for the missiles to counter the Soviet development of Gallosh Anti-Ballistic Missiles. This involved developing a range of 'new materials' to act as a 'screen'. While this area remains highly classified it is known that one of these materials was 3-Dimensional Quartz Phenolic (3DQP). According to one source, 3DQP is

> a phenolic-based material composed of quartz cloth material woven into a seamless sock shape cloth impregnated with phenolic resin and hot-pressed. The quartz material 'hardens' the Re-entry Body (ReB) protecting the nuclear warhead against high-energy neutrons emitted by exo-atmospheric Anti-Ballistic missile (ABM) bursts before re-entry. When cured, 3DQP can be machined in the same way as metals and is tough and fire-resistant.[1]

Welsh chemists played an important part in the development of the 'new materials' for UK nuclear warheads and in other developments designed to improve the reliability and safety of the UK deterrent force.[2]

Alwyn Davies, from New Quay in Ceredigion, was one of the key scientists who worked on the new materials. He was educated at Cathays High School in Cardiff and went on to graduate in chemistry from Cardiff University in 1961. After doing postgraduate and post-doctoral research at Imperial College, London he joined the staff at Aldermaston in 1969 as a scientific officer just at the time that the Polaris Improvement Programme was getting underway. As a member of the Chevaline project team he was directly involved in developing new materials for the hardening of the Polaris warhead. He worked in the Superintendency Weapons Chemistry division for several years, working on Chevaline materials and subsequently on new materials for the Trident warhead. He became section head of the analytical chemistry research group responsible for finding new methods for the analysis of the new materials for Trident and for the transfer of these new methods to the AWE Burgfield and AWE Cardiff facilities. He later became superintendent of analytical chemistry responsible for all analytical chemistry at Aldermaston. He was a member of a number of JOWOGs and SUBWOGs, working closely with scientists at a number of American laboratories, including Los Alamos, Livermore, Oak Ridge and Rocky flats. He was also responsible for the HQ nuclear weapons underground nuclear testing at the Nevada test site. As we will see later, he also went on to play a number of other significant roles in the MoD and in arms control negotiations in Geneva and Vienna.

Another of those involved was **Adrian Edwards,** from the Rhymney Valley, who was educated at Lewis Pengam Grammar School. He graduated from Aberystwyth University and joined Aldermaston in the late 1960s as a materials scientist. Like Alwyn Davies he worked on Chevaline and Trident materials and was part of the Chemical Technology Division. He was transferred to AWE Burghfield in the late 1980s and became the assistant director of materials research. He was also a member of several JOWOGs both in the UK and at various US laboratories.

TABLE 3 Anglo-American JOWOGs, 2001–9

Joint working group	Title
6	Radiation simulation and kinetic effects
9	Energetic materials
22	Nuclear materials
23	Warhead electrical components and technologies
28	Non-nuclear materials
29	Nuclear counter-terrorism technology
30	Facilities
31	Nuclear weapons engineering
32	Nuclear warhead physics
34	Computational technology
36	Aircraft, missile and space system hardening
37	Laboratory plasma physics
39	Manufacturing practices
41	Nuclear warhead accident response
42	Nuclear weapon code development
43	Nuclear weapon environment and damage effects
44	Methodologies for nuclear weapon safety assurance

Source: *Hansard*, 27 February 2009, column 1149w. There were many other JOWOGs and SUBWOGs apart from these identified in parliament (e.g. 12 Chemistry). New JOWOGs emerged and others disappeared as the requirements changed over the years.

Cliff Goode was another Welsh chemist involved in the Chevaline and Trident programmes. He came from Pontypool and graduated in chemistry from Swansea University in the late 1950s. He joined the staff at Aldermaston in the 1960s and worked mainly in the Analytical Chemistry Division, initially specialising in the use of neutron activation analysis/gamma-ray spectroscopy in a wide range of applications including applying the technique to the analysis of trace elements, often at the parts-per-million level, in materials used in the Trident warhead. After spending three years in Defence Science and Technical Intelligence (DSTI) in the MOD in London he returned to Aldermaston in the early 1980s as superintendent of analytical chemistry. In this role he was responsible for the analysis of various materials, including plutonium, uranium and beryllium. In 1989 he was appointed head of the Chemistry Technology Division. (He was replaced in both positions by Alwyn Davies.) He was also the UK principal to JOWOG 12b which dealt specifically with cooperation with the US laboratories on the analysis of warhead materials, especially Trident materials. He is reported to have been a very keen tennis player!

Colin Thomas was another of the Welsh chemists to have played a part in key research projects at Aldermaston from the mid-1960s to the 1990s. He was born in Cardiff and educated at Cathays High School. He went on to study at Cardiff University and graduated in chemistry in the mid-1950s. He worked in the chemical technology branch, eventually becoming section head, specialising in organic materials, including plastics and polymers. Like the others, he was involved in cooperation with scientists in the United States through the JOWOG system. His career paralleled that of **Gwilym Philips** who came from the Aberystwyth area of Ceredigion. Like Thomas he was at Aldermaston from the mid-1960s to the 1990s and became section head in the Chemical Technology Department. He was another member of a number of JOWOGs.

Brian Davies was another notable chemist who worked at Aldermaston. He came from Ammanford in the Swansea Valley. He went to Swansea University, graduating in the mid-1950s. During the period of nuclear testing he had responsibilities for analysing nuclear debris both from British and foreign nuclear tests. In the 1980s he was section chief in the Analytical Chemistry Division, working on the analysis of non-radioactive materials used in UK nuclear weapons. In the 1990s he was transferred to the office of the Assistant Chief Scientific Officer (Nuclear) (ACSA(N)) in London where he had the important responsibility for maintaining the 1958 US-UK Mutual Defence Agreement, under which the JOWOGs system was (and continues to be) conducted and which is at the heart of the Anglo-American nuclear special relationship. He was also involved with maintaining ACO 140 (the UK nuclear weapons classification guide) which is a highly classified document that gives guidance on all aspects of the UK nuclear weapons programme.

David Lougher was another Welsh chemist involved in the Polaris Improvement Programme. He came from Barry and attended Barry Grammar School. He joined Aldermaston in 1968 and worked with Alwyn Davies in the same laboratory on developing new 'screen' materials for Chevaline. In the late 1970s he was transferred to another part of the Chemistry division where he did secret work for the intelligence services. He is described as a man with a quiet personality, physically very slight, weighing no more than 8–9 stones.[3]

Another member of 'taffy's men' was **Ray Williams**. He was from Ferndale in the Rhondda and a contemporary of Alwyn Davies at university. He graduated in physics from Cardiff University in 1964 and went on to do research for a PhD from 1964 until 1970 (which was never written up). He joined Aldermaston in 1967, working initially on the hardened warhead for Chevaline and later as a material scientist in the Chemical Technology Division. He was involved in several JOWOGs. In 1990 he was transferred to ACSA(N) in London as assistant director responsible for the research programme in the post-contractorisation period. He was a particularly good rugby player, playing for the Welsh universities, Newport (then a first-class Welsh club) and for the Aldermaston rugby club. He was also a very keen squash player.

Although most of those involved in the various nuclear programmes were men, two women scientists from Wales also contributed to the work done at Aldermaston. **Pam Kurds** (later Hart) from Swansea joined Aldermaston straight from school in the late 1960s as a junior scientific assistant. She worked in the Analytical Chemistry Division under Alwyn Davies and they published a number of scientific papers together. She later worked her way up to a more senior management position in the 1990s. **Dilys Jones** (later Collins) came from Denbigh in north Wales and went to Cardiff University. After graduating she went on to do a PhD in the 1980s before joining the staff at Aldermaston. Like Pam Kurds she worked under Alwyn Davies in the Analytical Chemistry Division, specialising in particle size analysis.

Other Welsh scientists at Aldermaston in the 1960s to the post-Cold War period

Important work was also undertaken by Welsh scientists and engineers from a variety of different disciplines and specialist areas. These included Brian Thomas, Malcolm Jones, Kelvin Donne, Ken Morgan, Malcolm Chappell, Gerry Picton, Colin Waters, Terry Jenkins and Perllyn Thomas. As during the period from the 1940s to the 1960s, physicists and metallurgists were strongly represented.

Brian Thomas from Newport joined AWRE straight after graduating from Swansea University with a PhD in gas discharge phenomena in 1967. His early career involved work in the Optical Group on high speed photography and its applications to plasmas and upper atmosphere events. He was a founder member of the AWE laser programme, initially focusing on the development of diagnostic equipment for laser-plasma experiments. In 1973 he led a team carrying out these experiments and he also worked on laser-plasma interaction theory and target design. By 1983 he had become recognised as a distinguished scientist in AWE's Plasma Physics Division, concentrating on the design of laser targets for experiments that were intended to meet Aldermaston's requirements for improved understanding of high energy density physics. His work in the plasma physics area has been of considerable importance in helping to maintain and underwrite warheads for the British nuclear deterrent force.

Initially working with the Helen laser he went on from 2010 to work with the state-of the-art Orion laser. It is reported that Orion 'delivers a combination of ten "long-pulse" beams (a thousand millionth of a second in duration) and two petawatt beams (some of the most powerful laser beams ever created). The laser beams are directed into the Target Hall where the experiments are conducted in a 4-metre diameter target chamber operated at ultra-high vacuum.' The Orion facility allows scientists, like Brian Thomas, to conduct research 'into high density physics phenomena, which occur at the heart of a nuclear explosion or the interior of a star'.[4] His work in this area has involved research in the United States with US scientists from Los Alamos and

Lawrence Livermore Laboratories, and from 1994 to 1997 he chaired the Los Alamos Physics Division Review Committee. He then went on to chair the AWE think tank which covered all aspects of Britain's future nuclear force.

Although he officially retired in 2003 he continued to work part time at Aldermaston. In 2007 his major contribution to laser-plasma research was recognised by the prestigious Edward Teller Award from the Fusion Energy Division of the American Nuclear Society 'in recognition of pioneering research and leadership in Inertial Fusion Sciences and Applications'. At the time of writing he remains on the staff of AWE in a part-time capacity. In his spare time he has written a book of poetry entitled *It Struck Me* and, in line with his deep commitment to the land of his birth, he is engaged in writing a book on the history of Wales. He was awarded the OBE in 2001.

Malcolm Jones joined the staff at Aldermaston in 1967 at the same time as Brian Thomas. The son of a miner he was brought up in Nantymoel in the Ogmore Valley. One of his close friends while growing up was Lyn Davies who won a gold medal at the 1964 Tokyo Olympic Games. He graduated with a first-class degree from Swansea University in 1964 and went on to do a PhD in solid state physics before joining AWRE straight from university. In his early career he was involved in research and development into electronic aspects of nuclear warheads, including the electro explosive firing circuits. This work involved the design of the arming, fusing and firing architectures of the warhead. He later became involved in important work on the safety issues associated with the Chevaline Arming System and, subsequently, as a nuclear safety adviser to senior MoD and AWE committees, he provided advice on the contents of the UK's top level nuclear weapons safety standards, which remain in place today. He also set up the JOWOG group on nuclear weapon safety assessment methodologies and acted as chair of the group for more than twenty years.

With the development of the Soviet Galosh anti-ballistic missile system in the 1970s and 1980s an AWE group was set up to consider how these defences might affect the effectiveness of the UK's nuclear deterrent. Malcolm Jones was an original member of this group and had responsibility for overseeing the work on potential radiation effects on the Chevaline and later the Trident systems. The group also had a responsibility for making an assessment of the viability of the American Strategic Defence Initiative (SDI), known as 'Star Wars', during the Reagan administration. The advice provided by the AWE group on SDI was of major importance in the decision by the Thatcher government to express its concerns about the implications and viability of the American programme.

He also played a part in the technical studies leading up to the decision by the Thatcher government to procure Trident missiles from the United States in July 1980. In his words:

> Prior to the UK's decision to buy the Trident system I worked on potential high beta vehicle concepts including the requirements for fuzing options and this led to the development of the UK's first re-entry plasma code which was necessary for the assessment of radar interference. This led to closer collaboration with US colleagues who were then ahead in this field. I was also a member of the initial AWE party to visit the US and who were tasked to carry out a technical assessment of those parts of the Trident system which were being procured.[5]

In his career Malcolm Jones gave keynote addresses and lectures at numerous international conferences and represented AWE and the MoD at various events, including anniversary celebrations at Russian nuclear weapons design laboratories after the end of the Cold War. He also received an award from the All Russian Research Institute for Automatics for work he did on fostering nuclear safety. Other honours included the MBE and the John Challens medal, which is AWE's principal award for continued high quality lifetime contribution to science, engineering, technology and mathematics. In 2018 he was still working as an independent adviser on the safety of the UK's nuclear programme and as a panel review member engaged in advising AWE's senior management on the direction and needs for current and future programmes.

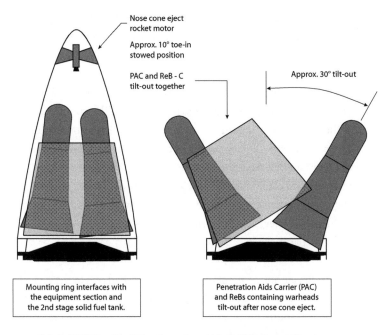

Nose cone eject
rocket motor

Approx. 10° toe-in
stowed position

PAC and ReB - C
tilt-out together

Approx. 30° tilt-out

Mounting ring interfaces with the equipment section and the 2nd stage solid fuel tank.	Penetration Aids Carrier (PAC) and ReBs containing warheads tilt-out after nose cone eject.

Polaris A3TK Chevaline PAC and re-entry vehicle (ReB) toe-in and tilt-out

FIGURE 6 Chevaline (by permission of Brian Burnell)

Malcolm Chappell, who came from Aberdare, was another physicist who graduated from Swansea University in the mid-1960s. Like Malcolm Jones his specialism was electronics and he also worked on the firing circuits of nuclear weapons, including the Chevaline and Trident systems. The 'fast track' from the Swansea University Physics Department was also evident with the appointment of another Swansea graduate **Kelvin Donne**. Professor Llewelyn Jones, Professor Grey-Morgan and Professor Thonemann of Swansea University's Physics Department had close links with Aldermaston and a number of their graduate students were appointed to positions at AWRE. Following his PhD research in computational physics of electrical discharges, Kelvin Donne was appointed to a position at Aldermaston in September 1977. He was told before he left Swansea to lose his Welsh accent by Professor Grey Morgan! He joined the Department of

Mathematical Physics where 'there was a significant Welsh influence'. In a note to the author he highlights the very impressive colleagues he worked with. In his words:

> Mixing with high flying theoreticians from Oxford, Cambridge, St Andrews etc transformed me as a physicist ... The atmosphere in the Department was similar to a research intensive university department, with a library just across the quadrangle. Lord Penney still had an office opposite to mine and occasionally popped in. Staff were expected to produce regular (internal) papers on their original research work and these papers also provided evidence for staff annual review boards – promotion prospects were very good in that department.[6]

In a note to the author, he points out that AWRE had one of the very first CRAY supercomputers in the UK, which was an indication of the high level of resources available to his department. He also expresses the view that AWRE was a tremendous asset to the UK scientific community and that its research was very highly regarded in the United States.

He also says that one of his great achievements while at AWRE was 'reaching the finals of the interdepartmental cricket competition and winning the only sporting trophy he ever won!' He left Aldermaston in 1982 to pursue an academic career. In 2010 he was appointed to a University of Wales research chair at Swansea Metropolitan University. He is currently Professorial Fellow at the University of Wales Trinity Saint David.

As the personal memoir below shows, another Welsh scientist, **Ken Morgan**, also found himself in a department targeted by recruitment staff from Aldermaston. In his case it was Bristol University. He also confirms the Welsh influence at AWRE. Professor Morgan later went on to hold a number of senior positions at Swansea University, and from 2008 to the present he has been Professor of Computational Modelling in the Welsh Institute of Mathematical and Computational Sciences.[7]

Personal memoir by Professor Ken Morgan

I was born in Llanelli in 1945 and I attended Llanelli Boys Grammar School. In 1963, I went to the University of Bristol and studied for a degree in mathematics. I remained at Bristol to study for a PhD in fluid mechanics in the Department of Mathematics.

In March 1969, AWRE approached the department and asked if there were any PhD students who were interested in working at Aldermaston. Although I already had a couple of offers from the Scientific Civil Service, I thought that AWRE sounded interesting and I arranged a visit. During the visit, I spent most of the time with Henry Pike, who was senior superintendent of Design Mathematics (SSDM). The SSDM group and the SSCM group (led by A. H. Armstrong) came under John Corner, who was chief of Mathematical Physics (CMP). Following this visit, without a formal interview, I was offered, and accepted, a job as a scientific officer with the UKAEA at Aldermaston.

I started work in CMP in September 1969 and I was located within the SSDM group. Alan Price and Peter Burgess were two others from south Wales in CMP at that time, who were both experimental officers. On my induction course, we had a talk on the Scientific Work of the Weapons Group by Dr W. G. John of SSWA. He was also a Welshman.

For part of my time at AWRE, I worked directly with C. Barham on design aspects. However, at this time, Aldermaston was very much into 'diversification', which meant that the major portion of my time was spent working with Nick Hoskin on the modelling of fast reactor safety problems. Nick Hoskin had undertaken his PhD studies under Sir James Lighthill at the University of Manchester and he had also worked closely there with Alan Turing. His modelling work with D. C. Cooper, later professor of computer science at Swansea University, was important in the analysis of the Windscale accident that occurred in 1957.

The UKAEA was building the prototype fast reactor (PFR)

at Dounreay and the CEGB had plans to start constructing a commercial fast reactor (CFR 1) in the late 1970s. These reactors were cooled with liquid sodium and we were looking at developing computer models for predicting the results of any fuel/coolant thermal interaction that might occur following a coolant blockage in a fast reactor core sub-assembly. The modelling work was accompanied by a large experimental effort at AWRE Foulness. John Rees, who was Welsh, was in charge of the Foulness work.

These activities were undertaken in collaboration with UKAEA staff at the Fast Reactor Design Office in Risley and the Safety and Reliability Directorate at Culcheth. We also interacted with other scientists at UKAEA and CEGB research establishments. One of these was Keith Roberts, at Culham, who had been a significant contributor to technological advancements at Aldermaston in the 1950s.

I left Aldermaston in 1972 and took up a position at the University of Exeter. I moved to Swansea in 1975.

Apart from physics, chemistry and mathematics there were a number of Welsh metallurgists at AWRE, following on from Graham Hopkin in the 1940s and 1950s, who did important work at Aldermaston from the 1970s onwards. **Gerry Picton** came from the Bridgend area of Glamorgan and attended Canton High School in Cardiff and later Cardiff University. He graduated in metallurgy in the mid-1960s and worked in the Metallurgy Department at Aldermaston on plutonium and uranium protection. He played a part in the metallurgy JOWOGs, working with colleagues in the United States and was seconded to the Defence Intelligence Service in 1980. He was also involved in the multi-million pound remedial programme on Aldermaston's radioactive facilities following the Pochin inquiry in 1978/9. This inquiry followed a contamination scare in 1978 when all the radioactive facilities at Aldermaston were closed down. He was a keen singer with the Newbury Choir.

Colin Waters was another metallurgist who graduated from Swansea University in 1975. In the late 1970s he joined Geoff Ellis's Metallurgy Department at Aldermaston, working initially on beryllium. He later moved on to work in the information technology and computer science fields. He moved to Burghfield in the mid-1980s and in the 1990s he joined the Defence Intelligence Service in London. And in 2004 he joined ACSA(N), taking over the secretariat of the Defence Safety Committee. He also had responsibilities for overseeing the Aldermaston warhead research programme. Like the others he was involved in a number of JOWOGs.

Terry Jenkins was from the Merthyr area and he also graduated from Swansea University and worked in Geoff Ellis's Metallurgy Division. For many years he was the officer-in-charge of one of the large production facilities, working on both enriched and depleted uranium and plutonium. During the 1980s and 1990s his group manufactured components for Chevaline and Trident warheads as well as for experimental devices used in nuclear tests. Terry played rugby as a young man and he was a keen squash player.

Perllyn Thomas from Glyncorrwg in the Arfon Valley was another Welsh scientist who contributed to the Chevaline programme in a rather different way. Thomas was educated at Maesteg Grammar School before going on to Swansea University to do a degree in mechanical engineering. Initially he worked as a graduate apprentice with Rolls Royce in its Aero Engine Division in Derby. He returned to Wales in 1971 as a quality manager with Zimmer Orthopaedic Ltd in Bridgend. In 1974 he joined Hunting Engineering Ltd (HEL) as the project quality engineer in charge of a team responsible for those elements of the Chevaline system for which HEL were the design authority. In 1978, 'as Head of Quality Engineering, he was responsible for Quality Planning and Engineering for Chevaline Production, Calibration Systems, Systems Audit and SQA Systems'.[8] Following this, in 1983 he was head of product engineering and in 1989 production manager with HEL, before joining AWE Cardiff in 1993 as general manager. AWE Cardiff played an important part in the UK nuclear story.

AWE Cardiff

The Royal Ordnance Factory in Llanishen, three miles north of Cardiff was opened in 1940 to produce tank, anti-tank and field guns. It was later used by the US Army to hold troops and undertake training in preparation for the D-day landings. In 1960 it became part of the atomic weapons establishment and began the production of non-fissile components for all UK nuclear warheads. With a workforce of 400 it developed the metallurgical capabilities 'for melting and casting, powder production, impact milling, ball milling, hot-pressing, isostatic-pressing and heat and surface treatment'.[9] The facility, in particular, specialised in producing high-precision components and complex assemblies, which included essential parts of thermonuclear warheads and beryllium/U-238 tampers for fission primaries. The Cardiff factory was also responsible for the servicing and disassembly of nuclear weapon components. In the 1970s and 1980s large amounts of depleted uranium and beryllium were stored and processed at the site. In 1987 a merger of AWRE at Aldermaston and the Directorate of Atomic Weapons Factories (at Burghfield and Cardiff) took place, and in 1997 AWE Cardiff was closed down. A number of the Welsh staff, including scientists, were transferred to Aldermaston.

Professor Sir Ronald Mason and the Trident decision

Although Welsh scientists and engineers made significant contributions to the Chevaline and Trident programmes, the greatest Welsh contribution to the decision to procure the Trident missile system at a high political level, and thus to prolong the life of the UK nuclear deterrent well into the twenty-first century was made by the highly influential scientist, Professor Sir Ronald Mason. Ronald Mason was born in Aberfan in 1930. He went to university in Cardiff to study physics and graduated in 1950. His first job was as a research associate with the British Empire Cancer Campaign from 1953 to 1961, which provided the foundation for the unique combination of science and medical expertise which was to characterise his later career. His move into academia came in

1961 when he joined Imperial College as a lecturer. In 1963 he became professor of inorganic chemistry at the University of Sheffield, a post he held until 1971. From Sheffield he moved to the University of Sussex where he was professor of chemistry until 1986.

As we have seen in the previous chapter Professor Sir Ronald Mason was appointed chief scientific adviser to the Ministry of Defence in 1977 and held the post until 1983. This role involved providing strategic management of science and technology issues in the MoD, specifically through the ministry's research budget of over a billion pounds. He was also a member of the Defence Management Board and the Defence Council, which were the two most senior management boards in the MoD.[10] As one of the joint authors with Sir Anthony Duff, deputy under-secretary of the Foreign and Commonwealth Office, Sir Ronald played a central role in recommending that there should be a replacement to the Polaris programme. The Duff-Mason Report, which was completed in December 1978, as we have seen, argued that the UK nuclear capability had four main purposes: as a contribution to NATO; a second centre of decision-making; as an independent force helping to defend UK national interests; and as a significant contribution to maintaining British political status and influence (at a time that her economic influence internationally was declining). As such the recommendation was that Britain should retain its nuclear capability and that Polaris should be replaced.

In a later interview he justified his support for a British nuclear capability in the following terms: 'The emotional security and political stability in this country entitle us to be a nuclear power.'[11] It is interesting that the Duff-Mason Report was opposed by powerful members of the cabinet at the time, including the Chancellor of the Exchequer, Denis Healey, and by David Owen, the foreign secretary. The prime minister, James Callaghan, and the chiefs of staff, however, supported the report, and, as we have seen, an informal approach was made to President Carter, to sell Britain Trident missiles, in January 1979. Carter was favourably disposed towards such a sale, but Callaghan lost the general election in May 1979. His replacement, Margaret Thatcher, supported the Duff-Mason Report, and used it as a basis for the decision to replace

Polaris. The report was discussed in the highly secret informal MISC7 committee and the decision to procure Trident was taken by the whole cabinet in May 1980. Given that Mason was responsible in the report for the technical options for replacement and concluded that the US Trident system was the best option, his role in this key decision, was of immense significance.

Professor Mason had an international reputation in the field of organometallic chemistry, spending periods as a visiting professor in Australia, Canada, France, Israel, New Zealand and the United States. His research focused on the study of bonds that form between metals and organic compounds. Apart from his role as chief scientific officer in the MoD, reflecting his expertise in defence matters, and especially nuclear weapons, he was the UK representative on the UK Commission of Disarmament Studies from 1984 to 1992, and chairman of the Council for Arms Control from 1986 to 1990. He also held the post of visiting professor of international relations at Aberystwyth University from 1985 to 1995. Also reflecting his expertise in medical matters, he was chairman of University College Hospitals Trust from 1992 to 2001. He was elected Fellow of the Royal Society in 1975 and received his knighthood in 1980. In 2010 he was one of the founding Fellows of the Learned Society of Wales.

Nuclear arms control issues

The involvement of Welsh scientists at a senior level in the development of nuclear weapons meant that their expertise was also in demand by the government on nuclear arms control issues from the 1960s to the 1990s. Ieuan Maddock had played an important role with his expertise in the seismology field in the negotiations that led to the Partial Test Ban Treaty (PTBT) in 1963. For Britain the priority to maintain an effective deterrent meant that testing remained a priority right up to the early 1990s and support for a Comprehensive Test Ban Treaty (CTBT) was secondary. By the early 1990s (following the end of British testing in 1991), however, with an effective deterrent force in place with the Trident system, British governments, and in particular the AWE, played an increasingly supportive role in efforts to achieve a CTBT, as noted in the last chapter. In the negotiations that took place in Geneva and Vienna, one Welsh scientist, Alwyn Davies, played an important role. As 'a poacher turned gamekeeper' he was a member of the UK delegation at the CTBT negotiations at the Conference of Disarmament in Geneva between 1994 and the signing of the treaty in 1996. The UK delegation was led by the UK ambassador, Sir Michael Weston. Alwyn Davies has described his role in the following personal memoir:

Personal memoir by Alwyn Davies

In the period 1994–5 I commuted about thirty times from London to Geneva sometimes for a day or two, sometimes for two weeks. The longer periods coincided with the meetings of 'tiger teams' who were international working groups of mainly scientists/engineers assigned to address technical issues on the establishment of a global nuclear test monitoring system of over 300 stations involving technologies such as seismology, radiation monitoring, infrasound, hydro-acoustics, electromagnetic pulse monitoring. At Geneva I had two roles. The first was to give technical advice to Sir Michael on the consequences of any proposals tabled on the UK's ability to maintain and develop its nuclear weapons capability. Obviously this information was highly classified and could not be shared with any other Nuclear Weapon States (possibly US excepted) and certainly not with any of the Non-Nuclear Weapon States. In this role I had to maintain close contact with the scientists and engineers at Aldermaston and continued to visit the site regularly. The second role, because I was from Aldermaston, was to participate in some of the 'tiger teams' especially those trying to develop a worldwide radionuclide monitoring system for both particulates and noble gases, both of which are released during a nuclear explosion. Also because of my experience ... with on-site inspections (OSIs) under the Chemical Weapons Convention I was also able to contribute to the development of the same for CTBT purposes. The CTBT was eventually opened for signature in September 1996 and one of the outcomes of the CTBT was the establishment of a new organisation in Vienna, Austria, to monitor a CTBT once it had entered into force. Thus a new organisation, called the Preparatory Commission, was created in early 1997 starting from scratch. The UK Mission at the UK Embassy in Vienna required a technical advisor and since I had been part of the UK delegation to Geneva, I was posted to Vienna in June 1997 where I remained for almost four years. My main tasks were a) to provide technical advice to the Ambassador (Dr John Freedman) to protect UK interests in the development of the Preparatory Commission, and b) to participate at a technical level in the various working groups associated with the International Monitoring System (IMS), the International Data Centre (IDC) and OSIs.[12]

Britain formerly ratified the CTBT in April 1997. To come into force, however, the treaty required that forty-four named states (including the UK, the US, Russia, France, China, India, Pakistan and Israel) had to ratify it and to date this has not been achieved. Only thirty-six of the forty-four have ratified the treaty. (China, the US and Israel have signed but not ratified the treaty; India, Pakistan and North Korea have not signed or ratified the treaty.) During the period since 1996 governments of both political parties have used supercomputers to model nuclear explosions to keep the nuclear force up to date and safe.

Welsh scientists at Aldermaston today

Some of the Welsh scientists who played an important part in the work on Chevaline and on Trident have continued their involvement with the work at Aldermaston through to the present day. This has been true of Malcolm Jones and Brian Thomas who, as distinguished scientists at AWE, continued working on a part-time basis after retirement. In 2005 the defence secretary at the time, John Reid, announced that the MoD would be taking forward a programme of investment in sustaining key skills and facilities at the Atomic Weapons Establishment. This was known as the Nuclear Warhead Capability Sustainment Programme (NWCSP). Retaining the skills of key scientists like Malcolm Jones and Brain Thomas was an important part of the NWCSP; the work on laser research conducted by Brian Thomas has been particularly so. Following the moratorium on nuclear testing at the Nevada Test Site announced by President George H. W. Bush in 1992 and Britain's ratification of the CTBT, the UK has not undertaken any further nuclear weapons tests. This has meant that it has been very dependent on an historic database of information derived from past nuclear tests and from a much more theoretical approach centred on modelling the behaviour of warhead materials and components at extreme temperatures and pressures. This has depended on the Orion high-powered laser facilities at AWE where Brian Thomas and his colleagues have continued to make a major contribution to the work being done on the modernisation and safety of the warhead for the Trident missile (the Mark 4A modified warhead) and the revamped nuclear warhead, known as the High Surety Warhead (HSW), which was a British version of the Reliable Replacement Warhead (RRW) which was under development in the United States.

Apart from maintaining the warheads for Trident safely and reliably and ensuring the capability to design future warheads, the contemporary responsibilities of AWE include work on decommissioning excess warheads in the existing Trident stockpile, following the government's decision in 2010 to reduce the number from 225 to around 180 by 2025, and also developing the skills, technologies and techniques that are necessary to support existing and future arms control agreements.[13] At present this involves a staff of around 5,000 in a wide range of scientific, engineering and administrative roles. Not surprisingly, the relative contribution of Welsh scientists and engineers is significantly less in the contemporary period than it was in the early post-war period when UK nuclear weapons were produced. Nevertheless, scientists and engineers from Wales are still making a contribution to the development of the UK nuclear deterrent today. These include Geraint Parry-Jones, Arfon Jones and Richard Jones. **Geraint Parry-Jones** was born in Bangor in 1963 and attended Ysgol Dinas Bran in Llangollen. He went on to study at Swansea University, and graduated in mechanical engineering in 1985. He joined Aldermaston in 1988 and currently holds the position of distinguished engineer. **Arfon Jones** is also from north Wales, from Cemaes on Anglesey. He obtained a first-class degree in chemistry and a PhD from Bangor University before joining AWE in 1999. He went on to do an MSc in electrochemistry at Cambridge while working at Aldermaston. **Richard Jones** was born and brought up in Swansea. He did his degree in physics and planetary physics and his PhD at Aberystwyth University . Geraint Parry-Jones, Arfon Jones and Richard Jones represent a new generation of Welsh scientists and engineers at Aldermaston who follow in the tradition of Ieuan Maddock, David Lewis and Graham Hopkin who were the pioneers of the early development of the British nuclear deterrent force.

Conclusion

As in the early post-war period Welsh scientists and engineers were involved in the three main disciplines at Aldermaston: metallurgy, chemistry and physics. Their contributions to the nuclear weapons programme covered a wide range of different areas, including special materials, warhead research and design, firing circuits, laser plasma research, the analysis of nuclear debris and intelligence matters, and arms control issues. Many of them were involved in the underground testing programme in the United States as well as the JOWOGs with American scientists and engineers. A number of them spent time working in American research laboratories. Like their colleagues in the 1940s and 1950s many were highly respected in the American scientific community.

Most of the Welsh contingent at Aldermaston were men but there were also two female scientists, Pam Kurds and Dilys Jones, who contributed to the important work done in the field of chemical analysis. Indeed it is noteworthy how many of the Welsh scientists worked in the Chemical Analysis Division, which a number of them headed at various times.

Despite their different disciplines the main focus of the work of most of the Welsh scientists and engineers (like most other scientists and engineers at Aldermaston) during the period from the 1960s through to the present day has centred on the Chevaline project and the warheads developed for the Trident missile, including the more recent upgrading of the W76 warhead and the Mark 4A re-entry vehicle. Both were major projects at the very heart of the UK government's continuing policy since 1945 of developing and maintaining a credible and highly sophisticated nuclear deterrent as the foundation of national security. They have also contributed to the important scientific work that has been undertaken at Aldermaston and its seismology team at Blacknest on supporting the arms control process from the PTBT and the Non-proliferation Treaty in the 1960s to the CTBT in 1996 and ongoing efforts to detect illicit nuclear testing.

7

CONCLUSION

During the Second World War the great breakthrough in the development and use of atomic energy for military purposes came with the Peierls-Frisch memorandum and Maud Report in Britain and later the Manhattan Project in the United States. Chapter 1 has highlighted the role played by two Welsh scientists in these momentous events. Eddie Bowen, a specialist in radar research, was chosen by the Churchill government to be part of the British Technical and Scientific Mission (the Tizard Mission) which was sent to the United States in August 1940 during the Battle of Britain.[1] James Phinney Baxter III, an American historian, has described the information provided to the US by the Tizard Mission as 'the most valuable cargo ever brought to these shores'.[2] Amongst the wide range of military secrets passed to the Americans was the information about the feasibility of an atomic weapon. This was passed to a number of top American atomic scientists, including Enrico Fermi. Although he was initially sceptical, the information resulted in the speeding up of the US atomic energy programme, leading to the Manhattan Project. As we have seen another Welsh scientist who had taken out US citizenship, Arthur Llewelyn Hughes, also played an important part in wartime atomic energy research in the US. Hughes was responsible for the development of a cyclotron at Washington University in St Louis which was taken over by the Manhattan Project, and he subsequently held the highly important position of assistant director at Los Alamos under Robert Oppenheimer. Bowen and Hughes, therefore, both, in their different ways, played a very influential role in the setting up and the subsequent development of the key US research programme which culminated in the Trinity test of an atomic bomb at the Alamogordo range in the New Mexico desert in July 1945.

A number of the leading scholars on the history of the UK nuclear deterrent have commented on the large number of Welsh scientists and engineers involved in the UK programme following the Second World War.[3] This was especially true of the early project to develop nuclear weapons in the late 1940s and 1950s. Following the 1947 decision by the Attlee government to develop an independent nuclear capability William Penney established a small team at Fort Halstead and later at Aldermaston. In Penney's team there were a significant number of Welsh scientists and engineers who played a very important part in the work which led to the first atomic bomb test in the Monte Bello Islands in October 1952, and in later tests that led to the development of thermonuclear weapons in the late 1950s. The most senior of these were Graham Hopkin, David Lewis, Percy White and Ieuan Maddock, who later became deputy director of Aldermaston. Welsh scientists at Harwell also played an important part in the nuclear programme at a senior level, including Lewis Roberts (who became director of Harwell), Brian Flowers (author of the 1976 'Flowers Report' on nuclear energy and the environment) and Walter Marshall (later chairman of the UK Atomic Energy Authority). Following on from them, as we have seen, Welsh scientists and engineers have continued to play a significant role in the UK nuclear weapons programme throughout its history right down to the present day.

One of the most important aspects of the British nuclear programme has been the close nuclear relationship with the United States, following the Mutual Defence Agreement in 1958. The main vehicle for this relationship was the close ties between British and American scientists and engineers in a range of Joint Working Groups (JOWOGs). Welsh scientists and engineers played a full part in these groups. Prominent in the exchange of nuclear-related information were Geoffrey Ellis, Alwyn Davies, Adrian Edwards, Cliff Goode, John Thomas, Gwilym Philips, Brian Davies, Ray Williams, Colin Waters, Malcolm Jones, Gerry Picton and Brian Thomas. Brian Thomas was particularly respected in

American scientific circles because of his work on plasma physics. He spent a great deal of time working with US colleagues at Los Alamos and was even chosen to chair the Los Alamos Physics Division Review Committee in the mid-1990s. The Edward Teller Award in 2007 from the Fusion Division of the American Nuclear Society in recognition of the major contribution he made to the inertial fusion sciences was a clear example of his distinction in his field.

It is not easy to establish why so many Welsh scientists and engineers have played such an important part in the development of UK nuclear weapons and the close nuclear relationship with the United States. Six explanations might be considered. First, science and engineering have had very strong historical roots in Wales. As the Scientists of Wales series (of which this book is a contribution) has shown:

> For much of Welsh history, science has played a key role in Welsh culture: bards drew on scientific ideas in their poetry; renaissance gentlemen devoted themselves to natural history; the leaders of early Welsh Methodism filled their hymns with scientific references. During the nineteenth century, scientific societies flourished and Wales was transformed by engineering and technology. And, in the twentieth century, Welsh scientists were influential in many fields of science and technology.

The Welsh atomic energy scientists and engineers of the twentieth century came from this very long and important tradition.

Secondly, there is a strong tradition in Wales in the value of education. The Workers Education Associations (WEAs) played an important part in Welsh life in the interwar and post-war periods, raising aspirations and enhancing the career prospects of many young people with a working-class background. Ieuan Maddock was the son of a miner, who was expecting to be a carpenter after leaving school. David Lewis, Colin Hughes, Morlais John Harris and Alun Price were also miners' sons. State help to go to university in the post-war period also contributed to the opportunity for many working-class children to achieve a better life than their parents.

Thirdly, the quality of education at Welsh universities was very high with internationally respected academics working in many of the key scientific and engineering areas. In Swansea, for example, the physicists, Professor Frank Llewelyn Jones, Professor Colyn Grey Morgan and Professor Peter Thonemann were particularly well known in their field. Jones and Grey Morgan contributed to solving important problems raised in the early atomic energy programme.[4] Thonemann worked at AERE Harwell and from 1949 to 1960 he designed and helped to build the fusion reactor Zero-Energy Toroidal Assembly (ZETA). He was head of physics at Swansea from 1968 to 1984 where his pioneering research on fusion inspired later generations of students. Chemistry was also strong at Swansea, Cardiff, Bangor and Aberystwyth, as was physics and metallurgy at Cardiff and Swansea. Many future scientists and engineers employed at Aldermaston and Harwell were educated at these universities. (It is perhaps of some interest that over half of the scientists and engineers identified in this study were either from Swansea or educated at Swansea University.)

Fourthly, and linked to the quality of Welsh universities, was the tendency for scientists and engineers already working at Aldermaston to recruit staff from their old universities at times when more special-ist staff were required. One example, noted earlier, was David Lewis, who, as an established member of Penney's initial team, returned to Aberystwyth University in the mid-1950s in a successful effort to recruit young PhD chemists to join the expanding staff complement on the bomb programme.

Fifthly, it has been suggested that geographical factors were at work. According to Alwyn Davies the attraction of joining Aldermaston in the late 1960s was a combination of the challenging work on offer at the cutting edge of his field and being close to home. In his words:

Two of the foremost sites were at Aldermaston (Berkshire) and Harwell (Oxfordshire), geographically not far from Wales. Thus interesting work, not too far from home may have been reasons why several Welshmen went to Aldermaston. With hindsight I think it is the reason why I joined UKAEA in 1969 as opposed to other job opportunities around the UK.[5]

A sixth and more pragmatic reason for some scientists and engineers joining Aldermaston was money. While the job itself and the excitement of the world-leading research facilities provided at AWE were important, the provision of housing for young graduates was very attractive. One Welsh scientist appointed in the late 1970s told the author: 'The benefit of renting at a reasonable cost an AWRE house for the first couple of years – it made all the difference in moving from South Wales to the S.E. of England.'[6] Also the financial rewards offered were regarded by some as an important inducement. This was particularly so, for some of the brightest and best scientists and engineers just leaving university after completing their PhDs. The starting pay for those who had achieved a first-class honours degree was higher than for other graduates and higher than many other opportunities offered by other employers. This was especially important for young graduates from some of the more deprived areas of Wales who came from less affluent working-class backgrounds.[7]

No doubt there are many societal and individual reasons why so many Welsh scientists and engineers were involved in the development of nuclear weapons in the UK. Whether the nuclear weapons that they helped to develop were responsible for keeping the peace during the Cold War and since remains a hotly debated subject. Many of those involved believed that they did. Others had some doubts and anxieties about the work that they did and continue to do so. It is possible to have different views about the morality and effectiveness of the UK nuclear deterrent force, but the fact remains that the programme has involved world-class, cutting-edge research in a wide range of disciplines, and Welsh scientists and engineers have played, and continue to play, an important role in this major scientific endeavour.

NOTES

Preface

1. See Philip Jenkins, *A History of Modern Wales 1556–1990* (London: Routledge, 2014), p. 305. A survey by the Welsh United Nations Association of public attitudes towards nuclear weapons in Wales in 2013 found a significant majority opposing the British nuclear deterrent force. See *www.wcia.org.uk*, accessed 28 June 2018.
2. See Martin Johnes, *Wales Since 1939* (Manchester: Manchester University Press, 2012) and Len Scott, 'Labour and the Bomb: The First 80 years', *International Affairs*, 82, 4 (2006). See also Sam Blaxland, 'A Swinging Party? The Need for a History of the Conservatives in Wales', *The North American Journal of Welsh Studies*, 8 (2014) and 'The Conservative Party in Wales, 1945–1997' (unpublished PhD thesis, Swansea University, 2017).
3. See John Baylis, *Ambiguity and Deterrence: British Nuclear Strategy 1945–1964* (Oxford: Oxford University Press, 1995).

Chapter 1

1. See *www.ucsua.org/nuclear-power/nuclear-power/how.nuclear-power-works*, accessed 28 June 2018.
2. John Dalton, *A New System of Chemical Philosophy*, vol. 1 (Cambridge: Cambridge University Press, 2010).
3. For a detailed study of the history of atomic energy research see Margaret Gowing, *Britain and Atomic Energy 1939–1945* (London: Macmillan, 1964), pp. 3–30. Much of what follows in this chapter is based on this source.
4. We now know that beta particles are not just electrons, but also their antimatter counterpart, positrons, which are positively charged. This, however, was not known at the time. I am grateful to Professor Charlton for pointing this out to me and for his advice on this section of the introduction.
5. The experiment was done under Rutherford's direction by Geiger and Marsden.
6. Gowing, *Britain and Atomic Energy*, p. 11.
7. Gowing, *Britain and Atomic Energy*, p. 12.
8. Gowing, *Britain and Atomic Energy*, p. 26.
9. Per F. Dahl, *Heavy Water and the Wartime Race for Nuclear Energy* (Bristol: Institute of Physics Publishing Ltd, 1999), p. 120.

Chapter 2

1. Niels Bohr and J. A.Wheeler, 'The Mechanism of Nuclear Fission', *Physical Review*, 56, 426 (September 1939).
2. See Lorna Arnold and Mark Smith, *Britain, Australia and the Bomb: The Nuclear Tests and their Aftermath* (London: Palgrave, 2006), pp. 1–2.
3. The six scientists were G. P. Thomson, Mark Oliphant, P. M. S. Blackett, James Chadwick, P. B. Moon and John D Cockcroft. 'Maud' was a code name designed to obscure the work of the committee. For the origins of this name see Arnold and Smith, *Britain, Australia and the Bomb*, p. 293. It was the result of a mistaken understanding of correspondence between Niels Bohr and Otto Frisch. This source also has a very good explanation of the importance of the Frisch-Peierls Memorandum, produced in the spring of 1940, which first explained the method needed to separate U-235 and the possibility of producing an atomic weapon.
4. Their estimate was that the material for the first bomb could be ready by 1943.
5. *www.atomicarchive.com/Docs/Begin/Maud.shtml*, accessed 28 June 2018.
6. *www.atomicarchive.com*, accessed 28 June 2018.
7. The Maud Report was shown to Vannevar Bush and James Conant, the new head of the National Defense Research Committee. It was they who initiated further studies which led to the Manhattan Project.
8. Arnold and Smith, *Britain, Australia and the Bomb*, p. 3.
9. Swansea University is used throughout the book to refer to University College of Swansea (1920–96); University of Wales Swansea (1996–2007); and Swansea University to date. Other Universities in Wales have also changed their titles at various times. The simple forms Cardiff University, Aberystwyth University and Bangor University are also used in the book.
10. Apart from the Frisch-Peierls Memorandum and the cavity magnetron, Tizard's briefcase contained information about VT fuses, jet engine designs, rocket designs, super chargers, gyroscopic gun-sights and submarine detection devices.
11. See R. Hanbury Brown, H. C. Minnett and F. W. G. White, 'Edward George Bowen', in *Biographical Memoirs of Fellows of the Royal Society*, vol. 38 (London: The Royal Society, 1992).
12. See also Rowland Wynne, *E. J. Williams: Ffisegydd yr Atom* (Cardiff: University of Wales Press, 2017).
13. See Neil Prior, 'Wales' role in the birth of the atomic bomb', 16 July 2015, BBC website, *www.bbc.co.uk/news/uk-wales-33540282*, accessed 28 June 2018. Chadwick was a Nobel Prize winner and was one of Britain's greatest scientists. He headed the British team on the Manhattan Project. Both Chadwick and Oliphant were members of the Maud Committee. Klaus Fuchs joined the Manhattan project together with Rudolph Peierls and was responsible for passing on the key secrets of the atomic bomb and work on the H-bomb to the Soviet Union. He was arrested in 1950. See Christoph Laucht, *Elemental Germans* (Basingstoke: Palgrave Macmillan, 2012) and Mike Rossiter, *The Spy who changed the world* (London: Headline, 2014).
14. Margaret Gowing, *Britain and Atomic Energy 1939–1945* (London: Macmillan, 1964), p. 221.

15. The contract for building the four prototype gaseous diffusion machines: a single cell unit, a double cell unit and two ten cell units, was £150,000. See Colin Barber, 'The Atomic Bomb Connection', and 'The History of Building 45', *http://www. rhydymwynvalleyhistory.co.uk/history-atomicbomb.htm*, accessed 28 June 2018.

16. Gowing, *Britain and Atomic Energy*, p. 222.

17. Alwyn Davies to author, 9 September 2016.

18. Alwyn Davies to author, 9 September 2016.

19. Quoted in Gemma Parry, 'Workers' Vital Role in A-Bomb Creation', *South Wales Evening Post*, 7 August 2015. See also Colin Barber, 'The Atomic Bomb Connection'.

20. Gowing, *Britain and Atomic Energy*, p. 256. The Mond Nickel Company was taken over by the International Nickel Company of Canada in 1929. It is currently known as Vale Canada Limited.

21. A. L. Hughes and L. A. DuBridge, *Photoelectric Phenomena* (New York: McGraw Hill, 1932).

22. Washington University Cyclotron Records, WUA00297.

23. Arthur Holly Compton, *Atomic Quest* (Oxford: Oxford University Press, 1956), p. 176.

24. *http://physics.wustl.edu/nd/docs/hughes.pdf*, accessed 28 June 2018.

25. Arthur Holly Compton's book, *Atomic Quest*, provides a personal narrative of someone who was at the very heart of the scientific programme in the United States to develop atomic weapons.

26. *St Louis Dispatch*, 3 August 1975.

27. *St Louis Dispatch*, 3 August 1975.

28. *St Louis Dispatch*, 3 August 1975.

29. Note to the author from Jane Hughes, 24 May 2017.

Chapter 3

1. A substantial part of this chapter was published in John Baylis and Kristan Stoddart, 'The British Nuclear Experience: The Role of Ideas and Beliefs (Part One), *Diplomacy and Statecraft*, 23 (June 2012).

2. The National Archives, London, UK (henceforward TNA), AIR 41/87, 'The RAF Strategic Nuclear Deterrent Forces', 1–2. Tizard chaired an ad hoc scientific committee set up by the Joint Technical Warfare Committee (JTWC), which reported to the chiefs of staff. Tizard's committee included J. D. Bernal, P. M. S. Blackett, C. D. Ellis and G. P. Thompson, all of whom were very distinguished scientists. Blackett and Thompson had been on the Maud Committee.

3. TNA, ADM 1/117259, 'Effect of the Atomic Bomb on Warfare', DNOR, 4 September 1945.

4. TNA, PREM 8/116, Hollis to prime minister, 10 October 1945.

5. See Matthew Grant, *After the Bomb, Civil Defence and Nuclear War in Britain, 1945–1968* (London: Basingstoke, 2010).

6. See J. Baylis, *Ambiguity and Deterrence: British Nuclear Strategy 1945–1964* (Oxford: Oxford University Press, 1995), p. 48. See also TNA, AIR 20/7063. The RAF in 1956, Report by the Future Planning Staff, 6 February 1947.

7. TNA, AIR 41/87, The RAF Strategic Nuclear Forces, 17.

8. TNA, PREM 8/115, Jacob to Attlee, 12 November 1945. Professor Blackett won the Nobel Peace Prize for physics in 1948.

9. TNA, PREM 8/115. By 1949 Sir Henry Tizard also argued against British nuclear weapons on the grounds that other vital areas of defence would be adversely affected and it was better to rely on the US to provide the nuclear deterrent force.

10. Margaret Gowing, *Independence and Deterrence: Britain and Atomic Energy 1945– 1952. Vol. 1: Policy Making* (Basingstoke: Macmillan, 1974), pp. 21–2.

11. It appears that Senator McMahon was not informed about the Quebec and Hyde Park agreements when he formulated his Bill for congress. See Gowing, *Independence and Deterrence*, p. 107.

12. Secrecy was an important part of the British decision. The decision to develop atomic weapons was revealed to Parliament obliquely in 1948. 'D' notices were used to prevent any discussion about these developments in the press.

13. Quoted in B. Cathcart, *Test of Greatness: Britain's Struggle for the Atom Bomb* (London: John Murray, 1994), p. xvi.

14. Gowing, *Independence and Deterrence*, p. 184.

15. James Chadwick and John Cockcroft had worked at the Cavendish Laboratory in Cambridge with Ernest Rutherford who had split the atom in 1917. See Graham Farmilo, *Churchill's Bomb: A Hidden History of Science, War and Politics* (London: Faber and Faber, 2014), and Cathcart, *Test of Greatness*, p. 16. Cathcart's book provides an excellent, detailed analysis of the scientific and engineering teams that worked on the bomb.

16. Cathcart, *Test of Greatness*, p. 20.

17. Cathcart, *Test of Greatness*, pp. 7–8.

18. Cathcart, *Test of Greatness*, pp. 46–7.

19. See Gowing, *Independence and Deterrence*. See also Lorna Arnold, *A Very Special Relationship: British Atomic Weapons Trials in Australia* (London: HMSO, 1987).

20. The Herod Committee was set up in 1948 to consider all matters relating to the introduction of atomic weapons into the RAF. This was followed by the Salome Committee in 1953 which dealt with the technical and supply aspects of the introduction of atomic weapons into the RAF.

21. TNA, AIR 41/87. Humphrey Wynn, *RAF Nuclear Deterrent Forces: RAF Strategic Nuclear Deterrent Forces: Their Origins, Roles and Deployment, 1946–49, A Documentary History* (London: Stationery Office, 1997), refers to two weapons having been delivered by the end of November.

22. TNA, AIR 41/87.

23. See Gowing, *Independence and Deterrence*, p. 209.

24. Quoted in Gowing, *Independence and Deterrence*, p. 183.

25. Gowing, *Independence and Deterrence*, p. 450.

26. Lord Moran, *Churchill, Taken from the Diaries of Lord Moran: The Struggle for Survival 1940–1965* (Boston: Houghton Mifflin Co, 1966), p. 580.

27. TNA, CAB 128/27, CC 48 (54), 8 July 1954.

28. TNA, CAB 128/27, CC 48 (54), 7 July 1954.

29. TNA, DEFE 4/70, Note by the First Sea Lord, 12 May 1954.

30. This was the view of Nigel Birch. See TNA, CAB 128/27, CC 48 (54), 8 July 1954.

31. TNA, CAB 128/27.

32. See J. Baylis, 'Exchanging Nuclear Secrets: Laying the Foundations of the Anglo-American Nuclear Partnership', *Diplomatic History*, 25, 1 (winter 2001), 33–61 and 'The 1958 Anglo-American Mutual Defence Agreement: The Search for Nuclear Interdependence', *Journal of Strategic Studies*, 31, 3 (2008), 425–66.

33. Interview with Harold Macmillan by the author on 28 August 1979.

34. Harold Macmillan, *At the End of the Day 1961–1963* (Basingstoke: Macmillan, 1973), p. 335.

35. Denis Healey, *The Time of My Life* (London: Penguin, 1990), p. 302.

36. 'Recollections of a Secretary of State for Defence', *Journal of the Royal Air Force Historical Society*, 31 (2004), 12. The 'second centre' role became a formal part of NATO policy under the Ottawa Declaration of 1974. NATO Documents Website, *http://www.nato.int*, accessed 14 September 2007.

37. TNA, CAB 165/600, Burke Trend to prime minister, 1 December 1967.

38. On strategic culture see Jack Snyder, 'The Soviet Strategic Culture: Implications for Limited Nuclear Operations', Rand Corporation, 1977, available from *http://www.rand.org/pubs/reports/R2154.html*, accessed 8 May 2011, Alastair Iain Johnston, *Cultural Realism: strategic culture and grand strategy in Chinese history* (New Jersey: Princeton University Press, 1995) and Jeannie L. Johnson, Kerry M. Kartchner and Jeffrey A. Larsen (eds), *Strategic Culture and Weapons of Mass Destruction: Culturally Based Insights into Comparative National Security Policymaking* (Basingstoke: Palgrave Macmillan, 2009). See also Alexander Wendt, 'Anarchy is what states make of it: The social construction of power politics', *International Organization*, 46, 2 (spring 1992), 391–425 and Alexander Wendt, *Social Theory of World Politics* (Cambridge: Cambridge University Press, 1999) for social constructivist arguments which offer further insights into strategic cultural approaches.

39. In 1949 there was some interest in concentrating production of atomic weapons in the US with a stockpile being kept in the UK. It is not clear if this approach would have been agreed by the government. Negotiations on the issue ended with the arrest of Klaus Fuchs.

40. M. Ceadel, *Thinking about Peace and War* (Oxford: Oxford University Press, 1989).

41. Cathcart, *Test of Greatness*.

Chapter 4

1. Margaret Gowing, *Independence and Deterrence: Britain and Atomic Energy 1945–1952. Volume 2: Policy Execution* (London: Macmillan, 1974). This comment was made about the team that produced Britain's first atomic weapons device in 1952.

2. Brian Cathcart, *Test of Greatness: Britain's Struggle for the Atom Bomb* (London: John Murray, 1994), p. 136.

3. The actinide series encompasses the fifteen metallic chemical elements with atomic numbers from 83 to 103. Naturally occurring uranium and thorium, synthetically produced plutonium are the most abundant actinides on Earth.

4. See Brian Eyre, *Lewis Edward John Roberts CBE. 31 January 1922–10 April 2012*, Biographical Memoirs, *http://rsbm.royalsocietypublishing.org*, accessed 28 June 2018.

5. The Anglo-Canadian project had been set up in Montreal after the UK failed to integrate the (French) Halban/Kowarski group working at Cambridge into the slow neutron group in Chicago under Enrico Fermi. Chalk River, 130 miles west of Ottawa, was chosen in July 1944 as the site of a heavy water pile.

6. Many at the time thought that Harwell had largely fulfilled its mission in laying the scientific and technological base underpinning the exploitation of nuclear energy.

7. Eyre, *Lewis Edward John Roberts*.

8. D. Fishlock, OBE, and L. E. J. Roberts, CBE, FRS, *Walter Charles Marshall, CBE: Lord Marshall of Goring*, Biographical Memoirs, Royal Society, 1996, *http://rsbm. royalsocietypublishing.org*, accessed 28 June 2018.

9. Fishlock and Roberts, *Walter Charles Marshall*.

10. J. B. Lewis, 'Reminiscences of the Nuclear Industry', note sent to the author on 22 January 2010.

11. Plutonium is a man-made element created when an atom of U-238 absorbs a neutron and becomes plutonium-239. For neutrons to be absorbed by uranium their speed must be slowed down by passing through a 'moderator' of either graphite or heavy water. The Bismuth Phosphate Process was used to extract plutonium from spent uranium fuel. Despite the Anglo-Canadian work done at the Montreal Laboratory during the war and the involvement of British scientists and engineers at Los Alamos, their knowledge of the metallurgy of plutonium was very limited at the end of the war. Plutonium had been used in the Trinity test and the Nagasaki bomb and it was recognised by the scientists who had worked on the Manhattan Project that plutonium was superior to U-235 for use in atomic bombs. The critical size of plutonium was less and it was more efficient as an explosive, weight-for-weight. It was calculated that a bomb would need ten times as much U-235 as plutonium to produce half the TNT equivalent. Margaret Gowing, *Independence and Deterrence; Britain and Atomic Energy 1945–1952. Vol. 1: Policy Making* (Basingstoke: Macmillan, 1974), p. 165.

12. Cathcart, *Test of Greatness*, p. 132.

13. Gowing, *Independence and Deterrence*, vol. 2, p. 468.

14. See John Baylis and Kristan Stoddart, *The British Nuclear Experience: The Role of Beliefs, Culture and Identity* (Oxford: Oxford University Press, 2015). In the meetings following the 1958 Agreement, US and British scientists, including Hopkin, worked closely together exchanging information about each other's nuclear programmes.

15. Harold Macmillan, *Riding the Storm, 1956–59* (London: Macmillan, 1971), p. 323.

16. Lorna Arnold, *Britain and the H-Bomb* (London: Palgrave, 2001), p. 73.

17. Note from Alwyn Davies, July 2016.

18. Other key members of Penney's 'top' team were electronics and instrumentation specialists Charles Adams, John Challens and L. C. Tyte; mathematician John Corner; physicist Herbert Pike; explosive specialists Ernie Mott and Bill Moyce; and blast expert Roy Pilgrim. Other important figures were K. W. Allen who was the senior superintendent of the Nuclear Research Division at Aldermaston and Brian Taylor who was a member of the Mathematical Physics Division.

19. See *The Biographical Memoirs of the Fellows of the Royal Society*, 37 (November 1991), 325. In particular, Maddock did some important work with oscilloscopes, as well as very high speed cameras capable of taking photographs at the rate of 500,000 frames per second.

20. Arnold, *Britain and the H-Bomb*, p. 73.

21. Lorna Arnold and Mark Smith, *Britain, Australia and the Bomb: The Nuclear Tests and their Aftermath* (London: Palgrave, 2006), p. 39.

22. Arnold and Smith, *Britain, Australia and the Bomb*, p. 71.

23. Cathcart, *Test of Greatness*, pp. 132–6.

24. Cathcart, *Test of Greatness*, p. 211.

25. Cathcart, *Test of Greatness*, p. 130.

26. Arnold, *Britain and the H-Bomb*, p. 73.

27. AWRE newsletter.

28. Tritium, a radioactive isotope of hydrogen, played an important role in the H-bomb design.

29. Arnold, *Britain and the H-Bomb*, p. 183.

30. The Grapple tests have proved very controversial for one family in Wales down to the present day. William Brian Morris from Swansea was a sapper in the army who was present at the tests at Christmas Island. While he was there, he went swimming and fishing and he died in June 1958 of leukaemia. His family has fought ever since without success to get recognition that the cause of his death was related to the test programme. See Liz Perkins, 'Quest to have H-bomb links to brother's death recognised', *South Wales Evening Post*, 2 July 2018.

31. David Lewis published *The Ultimate Particles of Matter* in 1959 based on articles he wrote while at Aldermaston. See *Ultimate Particles of Matter*, AWRE newsletter, July 1956.

32. Lorna Arnold, 'Percy White Obituary: Scientist who helped develop Britain's first atomic bomb', *The Guardian*, 16 January 2013.

33. Gary Gregor, 'Secret scientist at the centre of Britain's nuclear programme', *South Wales Evening Post*, 16 July 2016. See also Arnold, *Britain and the H-Bomb*, p. 73.

34. See *wikipedia.org/wiki/nuclear_weapon_design*; Donald McIntyre, 'Project Crystal: Lithium 6 for Thermonuclear Weapons', UK Nuclear History Working Paper, 5, (Southampton University); and TNA AB 6/1085, Letter from Penney to Cockcroft, 8 June 1953.

35. K. Harris and P. Edwards, *Turning points in solid-state materials and surface science* (Cambridge: Royal Society of Chemistry, 2008), p. 797.

36. These interviews with Alan Macfarlane took place on 29 November and 5 December 2007.

37. Note to the author from Professor Mike Charlton, 27 November 2015.

38. He went on to get an MSc in physics from Birmingham University in 1959.

39. Much of what follows is taken from an article by his son John Harris, 'Blast from the Past', *The Guardian*, 8 October 2005. The quotations are taken from this source.

40. For a detailed analysis of the Windscale fire see Lorna Arnold, *Windscale 1957: Anatomy of a Nuclear accident* (London: Macmillan, 1992).

Chapter 5

1. This chapter is based on an article by John Baylis and Kristan Stoddart, 'The British Nuclear Experience: The Role of Beliefs, Culture and Status (Part Two)', *Diplomacy and Statecraft*, 23, 3 (August 2012).

2. Similar conservative assessments of the destructive potential of American nuclear forces are to be found amongst the US defence intelligence and military community. This, it has been argued, is a feature of an organisational (or bureaucratic) frame of mind through its definition and solving of problems. William Burr, 'The Nixon Administration, the "Horror Strategy" and the Search for Limited Nuclear Options, 1969–1972', *Journal of Cold War Studies*, 7, 3 (summer 2005), 47 and Lynn Eden, *Whole World on Fire: Organizations, Knowledge and Nuclear Weapons Devastation* (Ithaca: Cornell University Press, 2003).

3. TNA, DEFE 13/752, Annex A to COS 45/72, 25 April 1972.

4. For the amount of damage required see John Baylis, *Ambiguity and Deterrence: British Nuclear Strategy 1945–1964* (Oxford: Oxford University Press, 1995), pp. 220–362.

5. Confidential correspondence, 7 April 2006.

6. Private correspondence with Sir Michael Quinlan, 23 October 2002.

7. John Baylis, 'British Nuclear Doctrine: The "Moscow Criterion" and the Polaris Improvement Programme', *The Journal of Contemporary British History*, 19, 1 (spring 2005), 53–65.

8. Private correspondence with Sir Michael Quinlan, 23 October 2002.

9. TNA, DEFE 44/115, Appendix 1 to Annex A to COS 1181/8/2/66 The Soviet Anti-Ballistic Missile Programme Outline Intelligence Report Covering Inception to September 1965, TNA, CAB 168/27, EF/D/01059, Robert Press to Sir Solly Zuckerman ABM/PENAIDS, 23 July 1970.

10. TNA, PREM 15/1359, Prime Minister Future of the Nuclear Deterrent, 27 June 1972.

11. TNA, PREM 15/1359, J. H. Petit to Lord Bridges, 7 August 1972.

12. This report into the Effectiveness of the UK Nuclear Deterrent by the JIC has been retained under Section 3(4) of the Public Records Act. TNA, PREM 15/1359, JIC(A)(72)30, 7 August 1972.

13. John Baylis and Kristan Stoddart, 'Chevaline: Britain's Hidden Nuclear Programme, 1967–1982', *Journal of Strategic Studies*, 26, 4 (December 2003), 141–2.

14. TNA, DEFE 13/1039, Meeting British National Criteria for Strategic Deterrence, 10 November 1975.

15. TNA, DEFE 13/1039.

16. For the 1972 assessment for nuclear deterrence see TNA, DEFE 5/192/45, The Rationale for the United Kingdom Strategic Deterrent Force, 25 April 1972.

17. TNA, DEFE 13/1039, Meeting British National Criteria for Strategic Deterrence, 10 November 1975.

18. It has been suggested by one senior official responsible for the development of Chevaline that these views ignore the fact that the defence would degrade to selective defence of their key assets. Confidential correspondence, 6 April 2006.

19. TNA, DEFE 13/1039, Meeting British National Criteria for Strategic Deterrence, 10 November 1975.

20. TNA, DEFE 13/1039, Chief of the Defence Staff to Secretary of State Soviet ABM Cover, 31 March 1976.

21. Denis Healey, the Chancellor of the Exchequer regarded it 'as one of my mistakes as Chancellor not to get Chevaline cancelled'. Healey, *The Time of My Life* (London: Penguin, 1990), p. 313. Healey reiterated this view in a 2011 interview for the BBC. BBC 'Document' website, 'The Bomb, the Chancellor and Britain's Nuclear Secrets', *http://www.bbc.co.uk/programmes/b00zdj01*, accessed 26 July 2011.

22. TNA, DEFE 13/1039, J. F. Mayne to Secretary of State Top Secret UK Eyes A Atomic Artificer, 18 November 1975.

23. TNA, DEFE 13/1039.

24. TNA, DEFE 13/1039, Top Secret UK Eyes A MO 18/1/1 Prime Minister Polaris Improvements, 18 September 1975. Mayne, as private under-secretary to Mason was not mainly responsible for policy advice.

25. TNA, DEFE 13/1039, J. F. Mayne to Secretary of State Top Secret UK Eyes A Atomic Artificer, 18 November 1975.

26. TNA, DEFE 13/1039, Top Secret UK Eyes A MO 18/1/1 Note for the Record Meeting British National Criteria for Strategic Deterrence, 27 November 1975.

27. Present at the meeting were Roy Mason (Secretary of State for Defence), Bill Rodgers (minister of state for defence), Sir Michael Carver (chief of the defence staff), Sir Frank Cooper (permanent under-secretary of state at the MoD), Professor Hermann Bondi (chief scientific advisor in the MoD), E. C. Cornford (procurement executive), Sir Edward Ashmore (chief of the naval staff), A. P. Hockaday (deputy under-secretary of state, policy), Victor Macklen (chief advisor, projects and nuclear) and John Mayne (private secretary to Secretary of State for Defence). TNA, DEFE 13/1039, Note for the Record. Record of a Meeting in the Defence Secretary's Office held on Thursday 27th May at 2.30pm, 1 June 1976.

28. TNA, DEFE 13/1039.

29. TNA, DEFE 13/350, P.S. to S. of S. The Case for 5 S.S.B.N.s, 19 October 1964.

30. TNA, DEFE 13/1039, Note for the Record. Record of a Meeting in the Defence Secretary's Office held on Thursday 27th May at 2.30pm, 1 June 1976.

31. TNA, DEFE 13/1039, RM to Prime Minister, 11 June 1976.

32. Private correspondence between Kristan Stoddart and Lord Owen, March 2006, shared with the author. See also the transcript of 'The Chevaline Experience and the First Trident Decision, 1967–1980', Witness Seminar held at Charterhouse School, Surrey, UK, 13 April 2007, conducted by the Mountbatten Centre for International Studies and the Centre for Contemporary British History.

33. TNA, DEFE 13/1039, Note for the Record. Record of a Meeting in the Defence Secretary's Office held on Thursday 27th May at 2.30pm, 1 June 1976.

34. TNA, DEFE 13/1039.

35. TNA, DEFE 13/1039.

36. BBC 'Document' website, 'The Bomb, the Chancellor and Britain's Nuclear Secrets', *http://www.bbc.co.uk/programmes/b00zdj01#synopsis*, accessed 26 July 2011.

37. BBC 'Document' website, 'The Bomb, the Chancellor and Britain's Nuclear Secrets'.
38. BBC 'Document' website, 'The Bomb, the Chancellor and Britain's Nuclear Secrets'.
39. BBC 'Document' website, 'The Bomb, the Chancellor and Britain's Nuclear Secrets'.
40. TNA, DEFE 25/325, Terms of Reference for a Study of Factors Relating to Further Consideration of the Future of the United Kingdom Nuclear Deterrent, undated 1978.
41. James Callaghan, *Time and Chance* (London: Collins 1987), p. 553. Callaghan, of course, represented a Welsh constituency, Cardiff South.
42. These were respectively, the permanent under-secretaries at the FCO (Sir Michael Palliser), the MoD (Sir Frank Cooper) and Treasury (Sir Douglas Wass), all of whom were coordinated by Sir John Hunt (secretary to the cabinet) acting as chair. For personal recollections of the Duff-Mason Report see also the edited transcript of the 'Cabinets and the Bomb' workshop, held at the British Academy, 27 March 2007. Available from *http://www.britac.ac.uk/pubs/review/perspectives/0703cabinetsandbomb-1.html*, 10 May 2008.
43. Lawrence Freedman, *Britain and Nuclear Weapons* (Basingstoke: Macmillan, 1980), p. 60.
44. TNA, DEFE 25/335, M. E. Quinlan DUS(P) to PS to Secretary of State Briefing New Ministers, 2 May 1979.
45. Bill Jackson and Dwin Bramall, *The Chiefs: The Story of the United Kingdom Chiefs of Staff* (London: Brassey's 1992), p. 385.
46. Peter Lavoy (ed.), *Nuclear Weapons Proliferation in the Next Decade* (London: Routledge, 2008); TNA, DEFE 68/406, Factors Relating To Further Consideration of the Future of the United Kingdom Deterrence Part I: The Politico-Military Requirement, undated August 1979.
47. TNA, DEFE 68/406.
48. TNA, DEFE 68/406, Factors Relating To Further Consideration of the Future of the United Kingdom Deterrence Part II: Criteria for Deterrence, undated August 1979.
49. TNA, DEFE 68/406.
50. TNA, DEFE 68/406, Factors Relating To Further Consideration of the Future of the United Kingdom Deterrence Part II: Criteria for Deterrence, para. 20, undated August 1979.
51. TNA, DEFE 68/406, Duff-Mason Part I, para. 23 DEFE 68-406 e21-1, undated August 1978.
52. TNA, DEFE 68/406.
53. TNA, DEFE 25-335, Duff-Mason Part II Annex A, para. 4, undated 1978.
54. TNA, DEFE 25/335, The Future of the UK Nuclear Deterrent, 13 August 1979.
55. TNA, DEFE 25/335.
56. TNA, DEFE 25/335.
57. TNA, DEFE 25/335.
58. TNA, DEFE 25/335.
59. TNA, DEFE 25/335.
60. TNA, DEFE 25/335.

61. TNA, DEFE 25/335.

62. TNA, DEFE 25/335.

63. Quoted in Peter Hennessy, *Muddling Through: Power, Politics and the Quality of Government in Post-war Britain* (London: Weidenfeld and Nicolson, 1996), p. 124.

64. Hennessy, *Muddling Through: Power, Politics and the Quality of Government in Post-war Britain*, pp. 123–7.

65. Peter Hennessy, *Cabinet* (London: Blackwell, 1986), p. 155.

66. CMND 7979, *The British Strategic Nuclear Force Texts of Letters exchanged between the Prime Minister and the President of the United States and between the Secretary of State for Defence and the United States Secretary of Defense, July 1980* (London: HMSO, 1980).

67. CMND 7979.

68. TNA, DEFE 25/325, Britain's Strategic Nuclear Forces: The Choice of a System to Replace Polaris, July 1980.

69. Jackson and Bramall, *The Chiefs*, p. 392.

70. Margaret Thatcher, *The Downing Street Years* (London: Harper Collins, 1995), p. 247.

71. Thatcher, *The Downing Street Years*.

72. Thatcher, *The Downing Street Years*.

73. Private interview conducted by Kristan Stoddart with Sir John Nott, 3 May 2006.

74. TNA, FO/93/8/466, Sir Oliver Wright to George Shultz, 19 October 1982.

75. *Hansard*, HC Debates 975–976, 11 March 1982. Private interview with Sir John Nott, 3 May 2006.

76. Michael Quinlan, *Thinking About Nuclear Weapons: Principles, Problems, Prospects*, (Oxford: Oxford University Press, 2009), p. 126.

77. Sir Michael Quinlan, 'The British Experience', in Henry Sokolski (ed.), *Getting MAD: Nuclear Mutual Assured Destruction, Its Origins and Practice* (Carlisle, PA: Strategic Studies Institute US Army War College, 2004), pp. 261–74.

78. Neil Kinnock had been a member of the CND since the early 1960s. See Len Scott, 'Selling or Selling Out Nuclear Disarmament? Labour, the Bomb, and the 1987 General Election', *The International History Review*, 34, 1 (2012).

79. Robin Day, *But with Respect: Memorable television interviews with statesmen and parliamentarians* (London: Weidenfeld and Nicolson, 1993), p. 248.

80. The Glamorgan Archives and the National Library of Wales hold interesting information about the Women's Peace Movement at Greenham Common. See also Jill Liddington, *The Road to Greenham Common: Feminism and Anti-Militarism in Britain since 1820* (Syracuse: Syracuse University Press, 1989).

81. Ann Pettit went on to run a tile factory in her home town. She spent three years on and off at the camp in Greenham. Sue Lent only planned to spend a day or so on the walk but soon decided that such was the spirit of the women she returned home to get her belongings and went on to complete the walk and became a founder member of the camp. She later became deputy leader of Cardiff council. Other Welsh women on the walk included Thalia Campbell, a 44-year-old art teacher from Cardiff, who had four children; Mary Millington from Cardiff, who spent a number of periods

in prison because of her activities at Greenham; and Sian ap Gwynfor, a minister's wife from Llandysul, who had two children. See 'Thomas, Karmen (*fl.* 1980–3), campaigner', correspondence and papers held at Swansea University, Richard Burton Centre, and Ann Pettit, *Walking to Greenham: How the Peace Camp started and the Cold War Ended* (Aberystwyth: Honno Press, 2006).

82. See '"Key" Role of Women from Wales in Greenham Peace Camp'. Available at: *www.bbc.com/news/uk-wales-14693265*, accessed 29 June 2018.

83. J. Ainslie, 'The Future of the British Bomb', WMD Awareness Program Web Page, *http://www.comeclean.org.uk/content/future_of_the_british_bomb.pdf*, p. 89, n. 474, accessed October 2005. They might at times even be carrying a single warhead.

84. Ainslie, 'The Future of the British Bomb'.

85. BBC News Webpage, *http://news.bbc.co.uk/1/hi/programmes/newsnight/3236374.stm*, accessed 6 September 2007.

86. CMND 6994, *The Future of the United Kingdom's Nuclear Deterrent* (London: HMSO, 2006).

87. CMND 6994, p. 17.

88. 'The United Kingdom's Nuclear Deterrent in the 21st Century', Speech by Des Browne MP, Secretary of State for Defence, 25 January 2007 at Kings College, London, *https://www.kcl.ac.uk,newa-archive*, accessed 29 June 2018.

89. *Lords Hansard*, 24 January 2007 (part 0002), column 1107.

90. CMND 6994, and see Quinlan, 'Thinking About Nuclear Weapons', p. 128.

91. There are bilateral US-UK protocols for consultation over nuclear use but they bind neither state to any form of veto. For more information, see the document collection at the National Security Archive Webpage, *http://www.gwu.edu/~nsarchiv/NSAEBB/NSAEBB159/index.htm*, accessed 6 September 2007.

92. Within this there is also an unstated rationale permitting its use through a nuclear guarantee of extended deterrence beyond the NATO area. In the early days of the Polaris programme, for instance, thought was given to a role east of Suez in providing a nuclear guarantee to India. TNA, CAB 164/713, P. Rogers to Frank Cooper, Deployment of Polaris Submarines, 11 November 1966.

93. CMND 6994, pp. 22–3. See also Kristan Stoddart, 'Britain, the Renewal of Trident and the Nuclear Guarantee to NATO', in Grégory Boutherin (ed.), *Europe Facing Nuclear Weapons Challenges* (Bruylant: Bruxelles, 2008), pp. 75–92.

94. *Lifting the Nuclear Shadow: Creating the Conditions for Abolishing Nuclear Weapons* (London: Foreign and Commonwealth Office, February 2009).

95. Quinlan, *Thinking About Nuclear Weapons*, p. 129.

96. CMND 7948, 'Securing Britain in an Age of Uncertainty: The Strategic Defence and Security Review' (London: HMSO, 2010).

97. *https://www.theregister.co.uk>2017/07/05*, accessed 29 June 2018.

98. *The Guardian*, 7 June 2016.

99. *The Guardian*, 7 June 2016.

Chapter 6

1. CMND 7948.
2. The author is very grateful to Dr Alwyn Davies for much of the information which follows about the role of Welsh scientists in the Chevaline and Trident programmes. This information was sent to the author in a series of e-mails in July and August 2016.
3. Alwyn Davies, 'Welshmen at Aldermaston', e-mail to the author, 29 July 2016.
4. *www.awe.co.uk*, accessed 29 June 2018.
5. Notes provided to the author by Malcolm Jones on a visit to AWE on 28 November 2017.
6. Notes from Professor Kelvin Donne to the author, 10 and 27 February 2018.
7. Note to the author from Professor Ken Morgan, 22 February 2018.
8. *Quarterly Newsletter of the Atomic Weapons Establishment*, April 1993.
9. *nuclearweaponarchive.org*, accessed 29 June 2018.
10. See 'Chief Scientist to the Ministry of Defence', in Wikipedia, *https://en.m.wikipedia*, accessed 29 June 2018.
11. *iWise.com Sir_Ronald_Mason*, accessed 29 June 2018.
12. Davies, 'Welshmen at Aldermaston'.
13. It is planned to reduce the number of operational warheads from 160 to 120 by the mid-2020s.

Chapter 7

1. R. Brown, H. Minnet and F. White, 'Biographical Memoirs: Edward George Bowen, 1911–1991', *Records of Australian Science*, 9, 2 (1992).
2. James Phinney Baxter III, *Scientists Against Time* (Boston: Little, Brown and Co., 1946), p. 142.
3. These include Margaret Gowing, Lorna Arnold and Brian Cathcart.
4. The author has been sent a copy of 'Notes on possible Swansea Physics links to the UK Atomic Weapons programme' by Dr Philip Prewett which highlights the work of the department on ionisation and its link to fast switches used in nuclear weapons. Dr Prewett also highlights the importance of Professor Peter Thonemann who became head of the Department of Physics at Swansea in 1968. Professor Thonemann had been the former head of the Zeta Project at Harwell and the first deputy director of the Culham Lab. Frank Llewelyn Jones had a major reputation in fields of ionisation physics and the physics of electrical contacts. He was Head of Department from 1945 to 1965 and Principal of the University from 1965 to 1974. Colyn Grey Morgan specialised in the areas of high voltage discharge physics, resonance ionisation spectroscopy and high density plasma physics. He played an important role in the early development of CERN.
5. Alwyn Davies, 'Welshmen at Aldermaston', e-mail to the author, 29 July 2016.
6. Note from Professor Kelvin Donne to the author, 27 February 2018.
7. This point was put to the author by a number of Welsh scientists and engineers he met during a visit to Aldermaston on 28 November 2017.

Appendix 1

WELSH SCIENTISTS AND ENGINEERS INVOLVED IN THE ATOMIC ENERGY PROGRAMME

1. Arthur Llewelyn Hughes – Liverpool University/Washington University, St Louis/Manhattan Project
2. Edward ('Eddie') George Bowen – (Swansea) Swansea University/King's College, London/Orfordness
3. Lewis Roberts – (Swansea) Oxford University/Harwell
4. Brian Flowers – (Swansea) Cambridge/Harwell
5. Walter Marshall – (Cardiff) Birmingham University/Harwell
6. Ieuan Maddock – (Swansea) Swansea University/Aldermaston
7. David Lewis – (Brynmawr) Aberystwyth University/Aldermaston
8. Graham Hopkin – (Swansea) Cardiff University/Aldermaston
9. Geoffrey Ellis – (Ammanford) Swansea University/Aldermaston
10. Colin Hughes – (Cefn Fforest, nr Blackwood)/Aldermaston
11. Percy White – (Swansea) Swansea University/Aldermaston
12. David Barnes – Aldermaston
13. Alun Price – (Gwaun Cae Gurwen) Aberystwyth University/Aldermaston
14. John Meurig Thomas – (Ponthenri) Swansea University/Aldermaston
15. John Lewis – (Swansea) Swansea University/Harwell
16. Aubrey Thomas – Aldermarston
17. Reg Owen – (Swansea) Aberystwyth University/Aldermaston

18. Bill Rees – (Swansea) Swansea University/Aldermaston
19. Reg Figgins – (Swansea)/Aldermaston
20. Gerald Davies – (Swansea) Swansea University/Aldermaston
21. J. D. Davies – Aldermaston
22. Alwyn Davies – (New Quay) Cardiff University/Aldermaston
23. Adrian Edwards – (Rhymney Valley) Aberystwyth University/ Aldermaston
24. Cliff Goode – Swansea University/Aldermaston
25. Colin Thomas – (Cardiff) Cardiff University/Aldermaston
26. Gwilym Philips – (Aberystwyth) Aberystwyth University/ Aldermaston
27. Brian Davies – (Ammanford) Swansea University/Aldermaston
28. David Lougher – (Barry)/Aldermaston
29. Ray Williams – (Ferndale) Cardiff University/Aldermaston
30. Pam Kurds (Hart) – (Swansea) Swansea University/Aldermaston
31. Dilys Jones (Collins) – (Denbigh) Cardiff University/Aldermaston
32. Brian Thomas – (Newport) Swansea University/Aldermaston
33. Malcolm Chappell – (Aberdare) Swansea University/Aldermaston
34. Malcolm Jones – (Nantymoel) Swansea University/Aldermaston
35. Kelvin Donne – Swansea University/Aldermaston
36. Ken Morgan – (Llanelli) Bristol University/Aldermaston
37. Gerry Picton – (Bridgend) Cardiff University/Aldermaston
38. Colin Waters – Swansea University/Aldermaston
39. Terry Jenkins – (Merthyr Area) Swansea University/Aldermaston
40. Perllyn Thomas – (Glyncorrwg) Swansea University/AWE Cardiff
41. Morlais John Harris – (Welsh valleys) Birmingham University/ Windscale

Swansea university staff

42. Frank Llewelyn Jones – professor of physics and principal
43. Colyn Grey Morgan – professor of physics
44. Peter Thonemann – Harwell and professor of physics
45. Neville Temperley – Aldermaston and professor of applied mathematics

Appendix 2

THE DUFF-MASON REPORT

Top Secret
UK Eyes A

D/DS12/15/6/6/3

<u>Note for the Record</u>

1. In November 1977, Ministers commissioned a study of the continuing validity of the Moscow criterion for the effectiveness of a British deterrent. After further discussion, it was agreed in February 1978 that a wider study should be conducted of factors relating to further consideration of the future of the United Kingdom nuclear deterrent. (The Terms of Reference are at E1 in D/SA12/15/6/6/5A).

2. A report was submitted to Ministers in three parts:
   a. Part I – The Politico-military requirement for a UK deterrent.
   b. Part II – Criteria for Deterrence.
   c. Part III – System options and their implications.

3. Parts I and II were prepared by an interdepartmental group under the chairmanship of Sir Anthony Duff, FCO – known as 'the Duff Group'. The MOD representatives were CSA, DUS(P) and D of DR(C), with DS 12 providing the Secretary. The papers are on D/DS12/15/6/6/4.

4. Part III was prepared by an interdepartmental working party on nuclear matters (NMWP) – under the chairmanship of CSA with DS12 providing the Secretary. The papers are on D/DS12/15/6/6/5.

Top Secret
UK Eyes A

The Study of Factors Relating to Further Consideration of the Future of the UK Nuclear Deterrent

Part III: System Options and their Implications

1. We were instructed to consider four areas of the terms of reference for the wider study of factors relating to the future of the UK nuclear deterrent:

   a. the operational and technical characteristics required by any successor system if it is to be effective in the strategic environment in the 1990s and beyond;

   b. the programmes of other nuclear weapons states (NWS) for the development of strategic nuclear systems; and other international developments, including especially those relating to arms control, and the extent to which they are likely to constrain our choice and influence our decision;

   c. ballistic missile (BM) and cruise missile (CM) options for a successor system (other than a wholly British BM system), and the timing which would be appropriate for the development and introduction into service of each system, given the estimated future life of the present force and any further development of it;

   d. resource implications.

   The Terms of Reference also provided that the study should be undertaken entirely within Government and that contacts with other Governments, which would reveal the existence of the study, should be specifically approved by Ministers. In view of the sensitivity of the study, we have thought it best to complete the preliminary work without seeking agreement to contacts with other Governments. This does however mean that our assessments of missile and warhead characteristics and of the costs of various options must be regarded as to some extent provisional. More generally, we have had to face considerable uncertainty in reaching a view on the implications of the strategic environment looking 20–40 years ahead: we discuss the implications of this uncertainty in more detail below.

2. We have taken our assumption about future criteria for deterrence from Part II of the study. We consider here only the capability needed to inflict 'unacceptable damage', in the terms identified there; and do not examine the other nuclear forces which might be required to ensure that there are not major gaps in our spectrum of capability (see paragraph 17 of Part II).

The Present Strategic Force and its Effective Future Life

3. In Annex A, we examine the framework in which the present Polaris force was procured and the limitations this imposes on our future freedom of action, the extent of our dependence on the US under present arrangements, and the likely effective future life of the present force. We cannot specify a single date when the present force will cease to be effective; but, for the reasons explained in the Annex, we cannot expect to be able to run on the present force far into the 1990s.

The Assessment of Candidate Successor Systems

4. To assess whether and at what cost each candidate system might meet the options for unacceptable damage, we need to consider:
   a. The number of detonations needed to achieve the damage levels set. This is a function of the nature of the chosen targets and of warhead accuracy and yield.
   b. The number of missiles to be launched to ensure the required number of warheads to detonate over the target. This depends upon the nature of any defences which have to be penetrated; and upon system reliability and the flexibility the missile may have for deploying its payload to increase effectiveness at the targets and penetration to them.
   c. The ways in which the required number of missiles might be deployed. Of key importance here is the assessment of the survivability of the system against pre-emptive attack.

In the following, we look first at damage criteria, then at the general effects of the likely strategic environment on b. and c. above, and then in more detail at the choice between particular procurement options and their international, technical and cost implications.

I   **Damage Criteria and their Implications**

5.   Part II of this study specifies the following alternative sets of targets for consideration:
[Section redacted]

6.   We have assessed the number of successful detonations required to satisfy these damage criteria, on alternative assumptions about warhead accuracy and yield: the result is at Annex B, Table 1.
[Section redacted]

II   **The Strategic Environment in the 1990s and its Implications**

7.   We cannot predict with certainty the strategic environment in the 1990s and later; instead we must try to identify solutions that may be least 'scenario sensitive'. The general framework will be provided by continuing US/USSR competition and the scale of Soviet defences will be set by the perceived US threat, within the constraints of any relevant arms control agreements. We can expect the Soviet Union to continue to deploy countermeasures against strategic attack, including the capability for pre-emptive attack on strategic bases, command and control facilities, and launch platforms as well as defences within the Soviet Union. We have paid particular attention to the Soviet threat to possible strategic launch platforms and delivery vehicles, but we recognise that other aspects of our capability, such as the adequacy of command control and communications arrangements, also merit further study.
[Section redacted]

9.   **Cruise Missile Defences.** Present Soviet anti-aircraft defences have a very limited capability against CMs to US specifications. But there are no overriding technical obstacles to the development of such defences, particularly given the relatively slow speed and long

flight time of strategic CMs; and Soviet systems with a potent anti-CM capability are feasible in the 1990s timeframe (see Annex C). There are also no 'in principle' difficulties in testing and exercising these defences, and thereby enhancing their effectiveness.

Arms control constraints on CM defences are unlikely. We can assume that Soviet deployments will be related to the size of the US force (a total force of at least 3000 missiles); and, while economic constraints may well limit the scale of these deployments and therefore their effectiveness against the US threat, they could be much more effective against a smaller CM threat posed by the UK. US ALCMs will also be only one element of a strategic triad, the other two elements of which might be used at the same time as cruise missiles. US expectations that an acceptable proportion of their cruise missiles will continue to be able to reach their targets, despite enhanced Soviet defences, cannot therefore simply be read across to the UK case.

10. Work on the assessment of probable CM losses to Soviet defences is at an early stage: but, as we discuss in paragraphs 10–12 of Annex C, preliminary indications are that more than 300 CMs could need to be launched in order to satisfy the specified damage criteria. While it is impossible to reach any conclusion now on exact numbers of CMs that would be required to overcome the defences, the important conclusion is that the choice of a CM delivery vehicle would represent a much more defence-sensitive solution than would be the case with a ballistic missile.

The Threat to Alternative Launch Platforms

11. We have assessed possible launch platforms in terms of their ability to satisfy the criterion that 'a UK strategic capability should offer a high assurance that it will survive a pre-emptive attack'. We recognise that this must involve subjective judgement since 'high assurance' is not quantified. Moreover, in practical terms vulnerability cannot be assessed in isolation since measures to increase survivability may have such other undesirable consequences for

the environment and/or public attitudes to the extent that they must be ruled out. In Annex D, we therefore address a range of factors. Our general conclusions are that all of the alternatives to a submarine platform must be ruled out, and that, even in the submarine case, there may be some growth in vulnerability in the next 30–40 years.

12. We believe that in order to provide a high assurance of survivability for submarine platforms:

   a. Our SSBNs should incorporate the latest technology from our attack submarine (SSN) programme; and they should have the capability for near simultaneous launch of their missile load.

   b. Submarine operating areas should be extended by adopting a longer range missile. A range of about 3000 nautical miles would appear to be the optimum; if range fell below this figure, there would be a case for increasing still further the redundancy in the system beyond the level suggested below.

   c. The minimum force level required to inflict unacceptable damage should be continuously deployed, which would require at least a four boat force (Annex D). But to provide a high assurance of survivability in the face of a growing Soviet ASW threat, there is a strong case for increasing the number of submarines on continuous patrol. To satisfy a damage criterion which required one boat-load of missiles while also allowing for survivability, a five boat force might be provided with at least two on continuous patrol. For a damage criterion which required two boat-loads of missiles, an eight boat force might be provided to give at least three on continuous patrol. The deterrent threat could then still be posed even if a boat on patrol were lost to pre-emptive attack. This survivability advantage would of course need to be set against the additional cost and other considerations; and exact force levels would need further study taking account of manning and support requirements and costs.

III. **Procurement Options**

13. US and French programmes for submarine borne missiles are described at Annex E.

14. **Arms Control Constraints.** We have considered how far scope for procurement of a successor system in cooperation with the US or France might be constrained by arms control considerations particularly arising from a CTBT and from SALT. Once a CTBT enters into force, further UK warhead development testing is presumed to be ruled out for its duration. Our assessments therefore assume warhead yields based on the state of UK knowledge expected to exist by mid-1979 (although it may be that under a CTBT regime we could expect to gain further knowledge of US programmes).

15. As to the implications of SALT agreements, the US Administration has stated that a SALT II Treaty will not prevent the United States meeting its obligations under the 1958 Defence Agreement (see Annex A); and we judge that it will not in itself close off any submarine-launched options for a UK successor system. It is more difficult to judge the possible implications of SALT III negotiations, covering inter alias unresolved issues from SALT II such as restrictions on CM range and deployments. A negotiation which embraced all 'grey areas' systems on both sides could raise fundamental issues about the nature and scale of any UK successor to Polaris; but a more limited negotiation might affect only particular system choices, such as certain types of CM. The 'grey area' question is under detailed consideration elsewhere, and for our purposes we have agreed that at this stage no candidate system need be ruled out on arms control grounds.

International Political Aspects of System Choice

16. We recognise, of course, that political factors will have an important general influence on the attitudes of our Allies and on our own assessment of our interests. We have therefore considered the likely

attitudes of our prospective partners, and of our other major allies, to collaboration on a successor system, as well as our own broad politico-military interests which needs to be weighed against the other factors bearing on system choice discussed below. Our conclusions are at Annex F, the main points we would emphasise are:

a. the US has made clear its continuing self-interest in the maintenance of our nuclear capacity and does not regard non-circumvention obligations in SALT as imposing a general restrictions on future assistance, but US concern for the strategic relationship with the Soviet Union and the political implications of SALT might well inhibit US assistance in any significant strengthening of a future British deterrent by comparison with the present Polaris force. From the point of view of our own interests, continuing Anglo-American cooperation would involve least risk for the maintenance of the US commitment to the defence of Europe.

b. Anglo-French collaboration could have political benefits in terms of the development of relations with our European Community partners. It would, however, involve greater risks for NATO cohesion than the Anglo-US alternative, and general political difficulties, given French determination not to participate in nuclear arms control. Our ability to collaborate with France on nuclear aspects of a successor system would, in any case, be constrained by our existing obligations to the United States; and the US attitude to such collaboration is uncertain. Some lesser form of cooperation excluding nuclear aspects could have financial attractions for France but might be politically objectionable. If, in view of these difficulties, Anglo-French collaboration were ruled out and a US system preferred, there would still be advantage in seeking an agreement with the US which allowed the development of Anglo-French cooperation in the operation and maintenance in service of their ballistic missile submarines.

c. There would be advantage in establishing as much independence as we can reasonably afford in the procurement and maintenance of a successor system.

Technical and Cost Aspects of System Choice

17. **Ballistic Missile Options.** We have examined three main options:
    a. TRIDENT C4 missile, with a capability to attack multiple targets (MIRV),
    [Section redacted]
    b. TRIDENT D5: MIRV capability
    c. FRENCH M4: Multiple warheads with some capability for target spacing, but not up to MIRV standards:

    If the US was unwilling to provide a MIRV weapon system or if Ministers considered it inappropriate, possible 'fall back' positions would be a de-MIRVED C4 system (although the feasibility of this option is uncertain), or a re-motored and modernised Polaris A3 missile using some Trident technology (possibly giving a range of some 3000 n.m). These would, however, represent 'UK unique' developments with clear drawbacks in comparison with the TRIDENT C4 solution above (although they could well be superior technically to the French M4).

18. In terms of their ability economically to satisfy the criteria, the US TRIDENT systems have a clear advantage over the French alternative: their MIRV re-entry system offers higher accuracy, a capability to attack separated targets, and superior penetration of ABM defences, At least one of these conditions applies to each of the alternative targeting options. The M4 could meet these options other than ...
    [Section redacted]
    ... but the total missile requirement would be greater, as Table II to Annex B illustrates. (We have not at this stage attempted similar calculations for the possible 'fall back' positions in the previous paragraph. But it is likely that they would offer a comparable capability to the M4: that is 16 missiles would be sufficient for criteria ...
    [Section redacted] ... but other options would involve higher missile requirements.

19. Our main conclusions on other technical and operational aspects of the choice between BM options are:

a. there are clear technical drawbacks in adopting a French system, since the technology is at least a generation behind that of the US. Moreover, the Royal Navy has substantial experience of operating US ballistic systems and none of French systems. Forecast missile range of the French missile of 2200 nautical miles (n.m) is marginal for strategic use in this timescale. Missile costs would be likely to exceed the C4 alternative.

b. As between the C4 and D5, the main difference is the D5's increased range (6500 n.m) compared with C4's 4000 n.m. This additional range is unnecessary for UK use and it dictates a much larger missile and therefore substantial extra cost of both the missile itself and the submarine to house it.

20. We have carried out preliminary studies of two main options for the configuration of the missile section of a future SSBN, based on:

a. the mid-body of the present Poseidon submarines. 8, 12 or 16 launch tubes capable of deploying missiles of the size of C4 might be incorporated in variants of this design (and submarines on these lines could also be suitable for M4); but it would be impossible, either initially or later, to deploy D5 or successive missiles of similar size.

b. The mid-body of the OHIO class submarine. 8, 12, 16 or 24 tube variants of this design would provide the capability for C4 or D5.

There are three arguments in favour of b. It would provide more flexibility to deal with a changing threat, avoid any risk that the UK would be left with a 'UK unique' solution almost from the point of deployment of a successor system, and it would also avoid possible additional resource and financial costs of updating obsolete technology as could be required under a. Against this, the submarine would be larger and more difficult to support; a D5 missile, if chosen, would post further support problems; there would be substantial additional cost (possibly some £750m for a five boat force); and we have evidence that the US will not move to an inventory entirely based on large missiles in large submarines. This area would require further study when discussions could be held with US experts to obtain more accurate information.

21. We have also examined a possible alternative, if not complementary, approach based on a relatively large number of cheap submersible vessels each deploying two BMs. This philosophy might have attractions if there were particular concern about the state of the Soviet ASW threat: but it has serious manning, support and command and control drawbacks.

22. In summary and subject to further detailed study, the best BM solution on technical and cost grounds appears to be a C4 missile, and a submarine with a modified Poseidon-type launch system, and the power plant (PWR2) being designed for the next generation British SSN. On this basis, it should be possible to deploy the first submarine of this class by 1994, assuming agreement was reached by 1981, and the order placed by 1986: but the scope for advancing this timetable needs further consideration. Follow-on submarine would follow at 12–18 month intervals.

Cruise Missile Options

23. Missile and submarine options are discussed at Annex G. We believe the realistic missile procurement option is purchase from the US. (The warhead would be UK designed and built).

24. As to the submarine, a purpose-built nuclear-powered cruise missile carrier of about the size of our present SSBNs might carry about 80 CMs. This would, however, be a 'UK unique' solution requiring considerable development effort, and there are serious doubts about its feasibility. (Inter-alia, the US have not, as yet, made a decision on production of sea-launched cruise missiles; and they have no plans for developing platform capable of multi-launching missiles from a vertical position). A programme, assuming as in paragraph 22 an agreement by 1981, would lead to the first submarine deployment at least one to two years later than the BM

alternative, because of the additional development effort required for the launch system.

25. As an alternative to a purpose built CM carrier, we have also considered the option of deploying CMs in our nuclear powered attack submarine (SSN). There are two basic options here. A next generation SSN could carry a total of 24–30 SLCMs if the whole of its planned anti-submarine and anti-ship weapons capability were removed. The SLCMs could be fired through the torpedo tubes in salvoes of 4 or 5, with a reload interval of 30–40 minutes between salvoes. This approach has two main drawbacks. First, in essence we should be providing dedicated CM carriers which were less cost effective than the purpose-built design in paragraph 24, since each SSN hull would cost about £200M. Secondly, the SSN would not have the capability for near simultaneous launch of its missile load which we have earlier identified as important in view of the Soviet threat (see paragraph 12s and Annex D).

26. An alternative approach would be to deploy SLCMs in smaller numbers (say 6–8 missiles) alongside the SSNs other capabilities. It might then be argued that the SSNs other roles would not be fundamentally impaired and that none of the cost of the hull need be charged to the strategic function. There are, however, important objections to deploying a strategic nuclear capability in this way. Assuming that every SSN carried some strategic missiles and that 75% of the total planned force level of 16 SSNs could be available when needed, the total number of SLCMs deployed would still be relatively small in comparison with our preliminary assessment of the missile requirements to satisfy the criteria, and with the missile numbers which could be deployed under a purpose-built option (a total for the force of say about 100 compared with 80 for a single dedicated submarine). Moreover, it might be difficult to achieve a high assurance of survivability if the force were deployed in accordance with its other roles in the early part of a conflict: but the alternative of holding it back so the strategic capability was

not hazarded would be incompatible with the SSNs' other roles (and the whole cost of the force should then really be attributed to the strategic role). Finally, there would be command and control problems in dispersing our deterrent capability in this way. We conclude that this approach has important drawbacks for a capability intended to satisfy the specified criteria for a strategic force. This is, of course, not to say there may not be a role for SLCMs in SSNs in the theatre nuclear role; which we touch on in paragraph 29 below.

IV. <u>Illustrative System Options to Meet the Alternative Damage Criteria</u>

27. On the basis of the damage and missile requirements in Annex B and the discussion of submarine vulnerability in paragraph 12 and Annex D, and submarine options in paragraphs 20 and 24–26, it would be possible to construct a wide range of options for meeting the alternative criteria. Some of the possibilities for a BM force can be illustrated as follows (the costings are for a 20 year life including running costs, but excluding the cost of fissile materials, as explained in Annex H):

   a. A force of four submarines each equipped with eight MIRV C4 missiles (total cost – £3850M) or with 16 M4 missiles (total cost – £4300M) could pose a continuous threat: …
   [Section redacted]
   … posture) (see paragraph 8 above) and by the development of the ASW threat.

   b. A force of four submarines each with 16 C4 MIRV missiles …
   [Section redacted]
   … but could be vulnerable to the development of the Soviet ASW threat (see paragraph 12 above). The total cost for a 20 year life would be £4300m.

   c. A force of five submarines each with 16 MIRV missiles …
   [Section redacted]
   … would provide a measure of insurance against the development of the Soviet ASW threat, as well as against accident or

support difficulties. Even if one of the two boats on continuous patrol were lost to pre-emptive attack,

The Force on these lines would provide a significantly more flexible and survivable capability than those at a. and b. above. The total cost for a 20 year life would be £5150M.

d. A force of eight submarines each with 16 MIRV C4 missiles ... [Section redacted]

... even after the loss of a boat to pre-emptive attack. The total cost would be £8 billion.

28. We cannot provide a similar set of options for the CM case since we have no similar basis for calculating losses to defences (see paragraphs 9–10 above.) Turning the problem round and looking at the capability bought for a certain cost, the figures would be:

a. 4 boat force, 1 boat continuously on patrol, £M3800 with 80 SLCMs

b. 5 boat force, 2 boats continuously on patrol £M4550 with 160 SLCMs

c. 8 boat force, 3 boats continuously on patrol £M7150 with 240 SLCMs.

Although we can reach no categorical conclusions on the effectiveness of these options, our earlier discussion of CM penetrability suggests that none of them is likely to provide sufficient capability on continuous patrol to match any of the damage criteria; they are therefore unlikely to compare in cost-effectiveness to the BM alternatives in paragraph 27.

A Combined Ballistic and Cruise Missile Force

29. The earlier discussion has concentrated on ways of satisfying the criteria using either BMs or CMs. By basing our deterrent on a single type of delivery vehicle, we run the risk that developments in an area of defences may render our whole deterrent obsolete. A system which involved a mix of capabilities in the dedicated strategic role might be attractive in providing some insurance against this risk, but we believe that it would be beyond our resources to

produce two types of strategic system. If, however, a BM force in the strategic role were complemented by a CM force – which could be submarine, ground or air launched – in the theatre role which also had some strategic capability, this would, in our view, provide some hedge against the possibility of accident or technological surprise affecting our BM force.

Resource Implications

30. It is fruitless to speculate on the precise implications for the defence budget of a decision to proceed with a successor system since the consequences depend upon assumptions made about the size of the defence budget 8–40 years ahead. Small variations in these assumptions produce large variations in the absolute sums available. But for illustration we can set the cost of a baseline option in the context of levels of defence spending on the lines of those envisaged for the early 1980s. The procurement costs for the five boat force at paragraph 27c spread over a 12 year period would represent about 7% of the total equipment programme over that time. Over a 20 year life, annual running costs of £120M a year would represent less than 2% of the assumed annual defence budget.

[Extracts from TNA DEFE 24/2122 Duff-Mason report on factors relating to the further consideration of the future of the UK nuclear deterrent Part III System Options, December 1978]

SELECT BIBLIOGRAPHY

Arnold, L. and M. Smith, *Britain, Australia and the Bomb: The Nuclear Tests and their Aftermath* (London: Palgrave, 2006).

Arnold, L., *Britain and the H-Bomb* (London: Palgrave, 2001).

Arnold, L., *A Very Special Relationship: British Atomic Weapons Trials in Australia* (London: HMSO, 1987).

Baylis, J. and K. Stoddart, *The British Nuclear Experience: The Role of Beliefs, Culture and Identity* (Oxford: Oxford University Press, 2015).

Baylis, J. and K. Stoddart, 'The British Nuclear Experience: The Role of Ideas and Beliefs (Part One), *Diplomacy and Statecraft*, 23 (June 2012).

Baylis, J. and K. Stoddart, 'The British Nuclear Experience: The Role of Beliefs, Culture and Status (Part Two), *Diplomacy and Statecraft*, 23, 3 (August 2012).

Baylis, J., 'The 1958 Anglo-American Mutual Defence Agreement: The Search for Nuclear Interdependence', *Journal of Strategic Studies*, 31, 3 (2008), 425–66.

Baylis, J., 'British Nuclear Doctrine: The "Moscow Criterion" and the Polaris Improvement Programme', *The Journal of Contemporary British History*, 19, 1 (spring 2005).

Baylis, J. and K. Stoddart, 'Chevaline: Britain's Hidden Nuclear Programme, 1967–1982', *Journal of Strategic Studies*, 26, 4 (December 2003).

Baylis, J., 'Exchanging Nuclear Secrets: Laying the Foundations of the Anglo-American Nuclear Partnership', *Diplomatic History*, 25, 1 (winter 2001), 33–61.

Baylis, J., *Ambiguity and Deterrence: British Nuclear Strategy 1945–1964* (Oxford: Oxford University Press, 1995).

Cathcart, B., *Test of Greatness: Britain's Struggle for the Atom Bomb* (London: John Murray, 1994).

Ceadel, M., *Thinking about Peace and War* (Oxford: Oxford University Press, 1989).

Compton, A. H., *Atomic Quest* (Oxford: Oxford University Press, 1956).

Freedman, L., *Britain and Nuclear Weapons* (Basingstoke: Macmillan, 1980).

Gowing, M., *Independence and Deterrence; Britain and Atomic Energy 1945–1952. Vol. 1: Policy Making* (Basingstoke: Macmillan, 1974).

Gowing, M., *Independence and Deterrence: Britain and Atomic Energy 1945–1952. Volume 2: Policy Execution* (London: Macmillan, 1974).

Gowing, M., *Britain and Atomic Energy 1939–1945* (London: Macmillan, 1964).

Grant, M., *After the Bomb, Civil Defence and Nuclear War in Britain, 1945–1968* (London: Basingstoke, 2010).

Jenkins, P., *A History of Modern Wales 1556–1990* (London: Routledge, 2014).

Johnes, M., *Wales Since 1939* (Manchester: Manchester University Press, 2012).

Jones, M., *The Official History of the UK Strategic Nuclear Deterrent: Volume 1. From the V-Bomber Era to the Arrival of Polaris 1945–64* (London: Routledge, 2017).

Jones, M., *The Official History of the UK Strategic Nuclear Deterrent: Volume 2. The Labour Government and the Polaris Programme, 1964–70* (London: Routledge, 2017).

Laucht, C., *Elemental Germans* (Basingstoke: Palgrave Macmillan, 2012).

Moore, R., *Nuclear Illusion and Nuclear Reality: Britain, the United States and Nuclear Weapons 1958–64* (Basingstoke: Palgrave, 2010).

Quinlan, M., *Thinking About Nuclear Weapons: Principles, Problems, Prospects* (Oxford: Oxford University Press, 2009).

Scott, L., 'Labour and the Bomb: The First 80 Years', *International Affairs*, 82, 4 (2006).

Simpson, J., *The Independent Nuclear State: The United States, Britain and the Military Atom* (Basingstoke: Macmillan, 1983).

Stoddart, K., *Facing Down the Soviet Union: Britain, the USA, NATO and Nuclear Weapons, 1976–1983* (London: Palgrave, 2014).

Stoddart, K., *The Sword and the Shield: Britain, America, NATO and Nuclear Weapons, 1970–1976* (London: Palgrave, 2014).

Stoddart, K., *Losing an Empire and Finding a Role: Britain, the USA, NATO and Nuclear Weapons, 1964–70* (London: Palgrave, 2012).

Szasz, F. M., *British Scientists and the Manhattan Project: The Los Alamos Years* (London: Macmillan, 1992).

INDEX